PRAISE FOR B

PRAISE FOR *AMBITION ADDICTION*

"There's the life you and I think we want. That's a sickness, really, and one that Ambition Addiction diagnoses thoroughly yet entertainingly. Then there's another life, a real, genuine, truly joyful life of service that you and I can lead. It's right here, right now—all it takes is the knowledge and presence of mind to face some very real facts. Shalva's book is bracing medicine for those of us caught up in the stress and hunger and busyness of this fast, fast world."

—Waylon Lewis, founder of *Elephant Journal*

"This is a well-written, hard-hitting book that will be invaluable for many people. Prescribed reading for those in the fast lane."

—Rick Jarow, author of *Creating the Work You Love* and *Alchemy of Abundance*

"Honest, funny, insightful, and full of integrity, Benjamin Shalva is a much needed voice in today's world."

—Chris Grosso, author of *Indie Spiritualist* and *Everything Mind*

PRAISE FOR *SPIRITUAL CROSS-TRAINING*

"A warmly told and deeply honest tale of one man's spiritual journey, filled with insight and wisdom gained from struggle and refusal to stop growing. This is a guy worth getting to know."

—Arthur Green, author of *Ehyeh: A Kabbalah for Tomorrow*

"Benjamin Shalva has written a beautiful, honest, heartfelt account of a lifetime of spiritual search. It can't help but resonate with all of us who have found ourselves searching through traditions, whether as spiritual dabblers or more serious cross-trainers."

—Benjamin Lorr, author of *Hell-Bent: Obsession, Pain, and the Search for Something Like Transcendence in Competitive Yoga*

AMBITION ADDICTION

OTHER BOOKS BY BENJAMIN SHALVA

Spiritual Cross-Training:
Searching Through Silence, Stretch, and Song

AMBITION ADDICTION

HOW TO GO SLOW, GIVE THANKS, AND DISCOVER JOY WITHIN

BENJAMIN SHALVA

Published by Grand Harbor Press, Grand Haven, MI

www.brilliancepublishing.com

ISBN-13: 9781503938632
ISBN-10: 1503938638

Cover design by Faceout Studio

Printed in the United States of America

For Lev and Avital,
my dreams come true

If you conquer all the world

yet lose your Self, all that you gain is

a wreath around your broken skull.

—Henrik Ibsen, *Peer Gynt*

I'm different. I have a different constitution; I have a different brain; I have a different heart.

I got tiger blood, man.

—Charlie Sheen[1]

CONTENTS

Introduction

Artists compete for top honors. Professionals yearn for promotions. Parents hope to raise little scholars with a laundry list of extracurriculars, and most of us wouldn't mind losing a few pounds. We have egos. We hunger for the good life. We dream.

This yearning for actualization, this burning desire to achieve—this is *ambition.* Ambition invites us not simply to survive but to thrive. Ambition tethers itself to imagination and possibility, allowing us to see present reality as raw material, raw material upon which we can improve. We locate a tiny seed of faith within, faith in our capacity to learn, to grow, to strive, and to triumph. We water that seed with our time and attention. We feed it with our courage. Slowly, that seed of faith sends roots into the earth and, defying gravity, spirals toward the sky. To our amazement, we grow. To our delight, we achieve.

For some of us, however, growth is not enough. Accomplishment will not suffice. Some of us need to distinguish ourselves from the herd. We desire domination. We ache for adoration. We want to win. Behind our eyes, a movie loops over and over again, a self-written, self-directed little piece titled *Any Day Now*. What *Any Day Now* lacks in plot, it makes up for in grandiose Hollywood endings. In fact, that's all this mental projection depicts—formulaic, saccharine, happy endings. Clichés abound. Depth and ambiguity don't make the cut. The hero wins. The world bows low.

Imagine a politician, a politician not only ambitious, not merely content to improve her life and the lives of her constituents, but ravenous for power and prestige. More often than she checks her Twitter feed, this Washington warrior's checking her *Any Day Now*. She imagines its glorious tableaus as she slogs through meetings and e-mails. Its happy endings urge her onward, dangling destiny before her eyes. *Any Day Now* greets her each morning and tucks her in each night. More so than any handler or aide, more so than any palm-sized device, it remains her constant companion.

If we could catch a glimpse of this politician's *Any Day Now*, if we could sneak into that secret cinema behind her eyes, what would we see? Her movie might begin with said politician standing on the steps of the US Capitol. Ever elegant, passionate, coiffed, and calm, she delivers a rousing speech for the headlines and the history books. A few moments later, her *Any Day Now* might shift to that same Capitol's west front. Facing the Chief Justice and a stiff January wind, our hero, a few years older (though from the looks of her perfect skin, it's hard to tell), takes the helm of the greatest empire on Earth. Cue the fanfare. Hail to the Chief.

If, instead of a politician, we screened the *Any Day Now* of an actor, an actor with sights set on global fame and inestimable fortune, we would see a very different film with the very same message. This actor's *Any Day Now* might locate him on a Broadway stage, bathed in light, dramatically reciting a stirring monologue. He performs with depth and grace, sweeping an audience of admirers toward revelation, lifting them in laughter, moving them to tears. Then, without warning, his *Any Day Now* might cut to the Dolby Theatre, where, standing beneath another set of lights, our hero lifts a gleaming Oscar high above his head. With a perfect blend of dazzled humility and Clooney-esque aplomb, he thanks director, producer, parents, and drop-dead-gorgeous spouse, a cascading tear sparkling in the light as it makes its way down his makeup-mottled cheek.

A stay-at-home parent's *Any Day Now*, focused less on professional achievement and more on paternal bliss, would nevertheless project just another variation on our well-established theme. This *Any Day Now* could open on a bright and spotless kitchen. Happy, healthy children, direct from central casting, eat a nourishing breakfast with knife and fork. Napkins cover laps. Smiles cover faces. Our protagonist, meanwhile, stands by the stove, surveying all this Rockwellian serenity with a fresh cup of joe in hand. Next, the film might cut to a shot of our hero cruising comfortably from morning Pilates to a lunch with friends. Life looks like a car commercial, our hero's SUV making every green light. Later that afternoon, our domestic dynamo arrives home to find the housekeeper straightening up and putting a delicious dinner in the oven. Suddenly, the front door bursts open. "Oh my God!" shouts the eldest son as he runs inside, a stack of mail under one arm, a number of opened letters raised triumphantly in his hand. "I heard back from Harvard, Princeton, and Yale. I got into all three!"

Any Day Now is no biopic. It never concerns itself with the day-to-day, year-to-year, often meandering, frequently disheartening road to stardom. It doesn't bother cataloguing minute wins and losses, nor does it make mention of developments or deteriorations in physical, emotional, and spiritual well-being. What did our hero learn on the path to stardom? How did our hero grow? *Any Day Now* bypasses all this holistic mumbo jumbo, skipping instead to the good stuff: the bright lights, the swelling orchestra, the wide smiles, and, most important, the all-encompassing win. These iconic images simply emerge from the void, rapturous, transcendent—liberated from laborious narrative and unencumbered by the slow passage of time.

Any Day Now is a lousy film. Yet, for those who freebase high-octane ambition, for those who wish not only to achieve, but to eclipse, artfulness is irrelevant. *Any Day Now*'s devotees can't go a day without running from the reality of their lives to this peep show in their heads They can't go long without at least a little fix. Especially when anxiet assails or depression descends, particularly when the sun hides all day behind a gray winter sky, all it takes is a quick peek at the screen behind their eyes. There they are—the hero! Look at their fame! Look at that success! Look at those abs! Who needs the sun shining above when such bright lights shine within? It could happen, it could really happen . . . any day now.

After every hit of *Any Day Now*, these emboldened individuals wipe the powder off their noses, check themselves out in the mirror, exit the theater, and enter the world. Sweet Lord, do they feel good! Hope and hubris course through their veins. Dreams of domination buoy them above the monotony of the moment. They charge toward their *Any Day Now* without a hint of hesitation. To prepare for that Broadway lead, they move to New York. To sculpt that bod, they hit the gym. To acquire that perfect spouse and those adorable, above-average kids, they date, get married, and get busy. Ambition addicts will attack their goals, whatever they are, with ferocious determination. And many will rise. My, how they rise.

Ambition addicts account for many of the manically productive and copiously accomplished individuals in our midst. They move mountains to make their dreams come true. And we, as a society interminably at war, dogmatically devoted to competition and conquest, inspired by the reality-TV maxim "I didn't come here to make friends," and obsessed with glitz, glamour, fame, and fortune, we respond to mbition addicts by pinning medals to their chests. We admire their racious appetites and go-get-'em attitudes. We shower them with rds, applause, and thumbs-up on social media. We boost their balng egos, encouraging them to vie for ever-rarefied stratospheres of ement. Our culture considers dog-eat-dog domination an unasright, the mark of mankind freed from the tyranny of code and and the shackles of social constraint. Ambition addiction does a great service, we argue, distinguishing übermenschen from the schleppers in our midst. Ambition addiction's not a problem. It the American Dream.

But ambition addiction *is* a problem. As ambition addicts grow dependent on this cycle of domination and validation, as they internalize the idea that their worth as human beings depends on the scope of their dreams and the efficacy of their efforts, ambition addicts will do anything to win. Some abandon their families. Others lie, cheat, and steal. The especially narcissistic, if given the launch codes, would happily crack the world in two, if only to feast on the Earth's sweet, candy center. A few famous addicts have already tried. Some addicts are trying at this very moment.

Most ambition addicts don't know they have a problem. They act believing that gold stars justify bad behavior. They let themselves off the hook, forgiving flaws and foibles as inevitable by-products of unparalleled greatness. Few think: "Hmmm . . . I stayed late at the office and missed family dinners for three months straight and it earned me that big promotion . . . maybe I should dial it back." Few worry: "Let's see . . . I viciously attacked my opponents, spread lies and suspicion, threatened whole swaths of humanity, and enraged entire quadrants of the globe and, as a result, I won the nomination . . . I'd better change my ways." When Hollywood tells an ambition addict's story, after all, the movie will feature a dashing leading man abandoning his pregnant girlfriend and then inventing the iPhone. Sure, it's too bad about the girlfriend and the baby, but the iPhone was worth it, right?

No—no intervention is coming. As long as society values unfettered, star-quality achievement over holistic well-being, ambition addicts will need to diagnose their own illness and administer their own cure. If they do so, when they dare to turn the wheel and ease off the gas, they may actually receive *negative* feedback. Their own minds will admonish: "What are you doing? Go for it! *Any Day Now* is just around the corner! Destiny awaits!" Others, likely those who have profited from their ambition, will cajole: "Where's your edge? Where's your

ɪed to be our 24-7, go-to guy!" Even the billboards along
ʋay and the advertisements popping up on every webpage will
ɛm: "Don't be a cog in the machine. Think different! Dream
ʃT DO IT!"

contemporary culture's imperatives fan ambition's flames, ambi-
ddiction is also kindled by a far more universal, ubiquitous source.
t ambition addicts, of course, have no knowledge of this source.
ʃhing toward their *Any Day Now*, ambition addicts keep their eyes
ed forward, glued to the prize. The root of their obsession, however,
ctually bears down on them from the opposite direction. What might
happen if ambition addicts shifted their gaze? What would they see if they mustered the courage to turn from their dreams and look back behind?

When ambition addicts allow themselves a quick glance back, they behold a terrifying sight. There, thundering toward them at breakneck speed, rush three of the fiercest, most ferocious predators known to man. Eyes narrowed to slits, lips stretched wide, fangs wet with spit and breath hot with hunger, these three pernicious foes track an addict's every turn. If ever an addict slows, this trio gains ground, preparing to pounce. Ambition addicts have been running so long, and have focused on *Any Day Now* so intently, that they've completely forgotten how, long ago, they embarked on this marathon not only to chase their dreams, but to outrun these pursuers.

Leading the unholy trinity is *Uncertainty. Uncertainty* barrels forward with shoes untied, kicking stones this way and that, tripping, falling down, then, with belching guffaws, picking himself up again. *Uncertainty* is cringingly unkempt; picture a hirsute, big-bellied, fifty-year-old man halfway through his first marathon, complete with too-short shorts, a sweat-saturated headband, and a skintight jersey. *Uncertainty* licks his lips and charges, arms outstretched, pits perspiring, eager to tackle an ambition addict at the least opportune of occasions.

Uncertainty's not exactly hostile, just unpredictable. Just when one thinks they've made something of themselves, right at the moment when one's got it all figured out, *Uncertainty* crashes through the screen door bearing yet another lamentable mess. *Uncertainty* calls at the office to announce that little Joey's got lice. *Uncertainty* pops out of the dash with our air bag, offering that shit-eating grin as life goes up in smoke. "Why now?!" one laments. *Uncertainty* answers with naive puppy eyes. "Can I catch a break, for God's sake?!" one bemoans. *Uncertainty*'s lost interest. He's ambled to the door to welcome in the tax auditor for tea.

Right behind *Uncertainty* is *Vulnerability*. This penultimate pursuer huffs and puffs, eager to bestow upon ambition addicts the longest, most uncomfortable hug of their lives. Here an addict goes, armed with a dream and a latte, ready to conquer the world. There *Vulnerability* follows, waving a stack of the addict's baby pictures, kvelling over those once-delicious thunder thighs. *Vulnerability* looks like a parent or caretaker, like someone who changed an addict's diapers when they were a gurgling, drooling dependent. Every time she catches up, *Vulnerability* squeezes an addict to her bosom and launches into stories they desperately don't want to hear, like the time the cat died, or that extended period of bed-wetting, or the time the addict stood cowering in the corner at the middle school dance. The more pathetic the tale, the more often *Vulnerability* tells it, pairing just the right Rosebud to an ambition addict's Kane. She speaks and an addict can't help but remember. She whispers and an addict stumbles, spilling the latte and wiping away tears.

Vulnerability's also got new tales to tell. While an ambition addict spends yet another late night at the office, she shows up with a picture of the addict's sleeping children. "Look at those little angels," she says. "Your youngest cried himself to sleep tonight. They must really miss you." When ambition addicts jump for joy, celebrating a latest triumph, she hands them the front-page news. "What a world," she sighs, "another day, another disaster. Do our victories really matter, compared with all this misery?" *Vulnerability* saps the wind from our sails. She's an expert at undermining momentum. And she does it all with a patronizing smile, as if she knows what an ambition addict doesn't know; as if she's noticed that the addict, on the way to the throne, wears no clothes.

A few paces behind irritating *Uncertainty* and incorrigible *Vulnerability* approaches a third sinister foe. When we look closely, this shadowy visage reminds us of the Ghost of Christmas Yet to Come, a specter "shrouded in a deep black garment, which concealed its head, its face, its form."[2] However, unlike a Dickensian apparition, this final pursuer has no intention to scare anyone straight. It views both charity and culpability with callous detachment. It could care less whether an addict eases off the gas or aims for an Oscar. Indifferent, inexorable, and inexhaustible, it is *Mortality*, and it will follow an addict to the stars and back, waiting for just the right moment to strike.

At the dawn of each new day, ambition addicts awake to find *Uncertainty, Vulnerability, and Mortality* looming over them. Rather than respond by groaning and grabbing a cup of coffee, or by pulling a lover close and burying fear beneath a blanket of warm, soft skin, or by taking a deep breath, offering a comforting prayer, and, rising to their feet, giving these demons a gentle nod before bravely facing the day, ambition addicts respond to *Uncertainty, Vulnerability, and Mortality* by looking for a way out. At some point, long ago, perhaps at a very young age, they grew sick and tired of sharing their space with these circadian callers. Addicts learned to open their eyes each morning and, before panic could incapacitate them, to leap out of bed and look for an exit, breathlessly searching for sanctuary from the human condition. They devoted their lives to putting their demons behind them forever.

And then, one day, they saw it. There, in the distance, a theater marquee, a beacon of hope shining through the early morning fog. For the very first time, they spied their salvation, immaculately encapsulated in three monosyllables: *Any. Day. Now.*

Uncertainty, Vulnerability, and Mortality give birth to *Any Day Now*. Were it not for this trio in hot pursuit, ambition addicts would have had no impetus to invent their movie. They would never have retreated into fantasy. We human beings are uncertain, vulnerable, and mortal creatures. For ambition addicts, *Any Day Now* serves as the one conceivable shelter from this existential storm.

Everyone, everywhere, sits in this same boat, confronted by these same demons. Yet, our reactions to *Uncertainty, Vulnerability, and Mortality* vary. Some will keep running the rest of their lives. Others, by nature or by nurture, keep it slow without the lows. They know how to take life breath by breath. They, too, have hopes and dreams, yet even with *Uncertainty, Vulnerability, and Mortality* breathing down their necks, they somehow keep their cool. They stay positive and present. They don't endure. They enjoy.

I actually met a number of these infuriatingly enviable individuals in, no big surprise, rural Nepal. I once spent three weeks, at the onset of monsoon season, slogging along Nepal's Annapurna Circuit. As the skies issued temperate samples of the torrents to come, as I splashed along in my not-quite-waterproof boots and forest-green poncho, I began to notice a fascinating phenomenon. On virtually every covered porch of every trailside home, villagers squatted still and silent, butts hovering an inch from the ground, knees jackknifed toward the thick clouds above. As I'd pass by, I'd offer each a wave. Each answered with a wide, toothy smile. Then, each returned to this motionless squatting, eyes on the rain and the gray haze beyond.

I asked a few Nepalis about all this squatting. They explained that a lot of these squatters worked as porters. The rest of the year, they shouldered huge bundles up, down, and around Annapurna's unpaved, boulder-strewn roads. During monsoon season, however, their work proved untenable. Tourism slowed, drastically reducing the demand for fresh supplies from the lowlands. The roads turned treacherous, especially for porters, most of whom hauled hundreds of pounds wearing their only pair of shoes: thin, plastic-strapped, smooth-soled flip-flops. So, with nothing to do and nowhere to go, these porters stopped, popped a squat, and waited. That was it. For three months, they watched. They waved. They waited.

Were they happy? I wondered this as I wandered past. They didn't look happy, exactly, but they didn't look unhappy, either. I didn't see anyone singing in the rain, but I didn't see anyone nervously pacing their porch or pulling out their hair. Were they happy? I couldn't tell, but perhaps that wasn't the point. Happy or not, these squatters breathed easy. They radiated an air of availability. They nodded and smiled and, if I started a conversation, seemed up for a chat. They lived uncertain, vulnerable, mortal lives, filled with their own unique blend of joys and sorrows; yet, stuck on a porch for three months of rain, they didn't run for their lives. They learned to live with their demons, nice and easy, day by day, breath by breath.

For ambition addicts, however, finding peace with both the rainy months and the sunny days can be an incredibly confusing and counterintuitive process. To exchange *Any Day Now* for this day now, ambition addicts must subdue their own impulses and turn to face their demons, demons they've spent the majority of their lives expertly evading. They must do so, also, while swimming against the cultural tide. Most ambition addicts don't live in a world of serene schleppers and sedate squatters. Just when they could use a seasoned sponsor, a fellow traveler to assist them on the road to recovery, ambition addicts may feel disparaged, discouraged, and utterly alone.

That's where I come in. My name is Benjamin Shalva. I am an ambition addict.

My family and I live in a safe neighborhood in a prosperous area of a vibrant American metropolis. I hold a number of advanced degrees. As a freelance writer, rabbi, meditation teacher, and yoga instructor, I'm my own boss and I make my own schedule. I have enough money to buy a cup of coffee at my favorite café every morning and to go out to dinner every few weeks with my wife. Our children go to a good school. I get to wear jeans and a T-shirt almost every day. That might not be your thing, but it's definitely mine. I feel needed. I feel loved. I'm surrounded by blessings.

But there's a part of me that imagines all this as prelude.

Enter the darkened theater behind my eyes, and you will see, up there on the screen, a suave Semite with soft, brown eyes and a well-groomed, dark beard standing behind a lectern in a crowded corner of a bookstore. A standing-room-only crowd surrounds him on three sides. He reads from a book cradled in his hands, and though you can't make out the title, you can see the words "International Bestseller" printed across the book jacket. He finishes reading to thunderous applause and then proceeds to answer questions from the audience. The camera zooms in on the faces of this adoring crowd. Wide eyes and bright smiles. Bodies edging ever closer. Everyone high on his wild, wonderful words.

Oh wait—the latest in CGI effects have seamlessly shifted the setting. Now that same man's enthusiastically bounding around a giant studio space wearing only linen yoga pants. He's svelte and sexy. The bulge of a huge, thick, power penis gently thuds against the inner wall of his briefs. He calls out eloquent instructions to the sea of bodies surrounding him. They bend and bow, smile and sweat, collapse, cry, and rise up in joy. Background music—sitar and tabla—swells to crescendo. One can smell the incense in the air.

Then the scene changes one last time. Our hero now walks through the streets of Brooklyn (or is it Berkeley?), with his wife and two children. His wife is beautiful, sexy without pretension, her long, untamed curls cascading over neck and shoulders. She's dressed in an outfit of organic cotton and floats down the street in Birkenstocks, occasionally glancing up at the man with small dashes of desire. The children laugh and dance around this couple, occasionally breaking away to run after their dog. Yes, there's a dog. A dependably obedient Norwegian elkhound who, despite her thick coat of soft, silver hair, never sheds.

A few minutes more and the family's made its way back to their hybrid station wagon. They climb in and set the onboard GPS for their favorite restaurant, a little hole-in-the-wall specializing in organic vegetarian fare. Just before the man presses the gas pedal, three beautiful, starry-eyed coeds run up to the car from across the street. They're big fans. Would he pose for a picture and sign some autographs? He smiles generously, puts the car into park, and climbs out. Duty calls. After these star-struck sirens wave good-bye, each posting their serendipity to social media, he climbs back in the car. A classic rock ballad begins to play. Then the camera pans out, the station wagon rolls toward the horizon, and the movie fades to black.

This *Any Day Now* plays in my head each and every day. Sometimes each and every hour. I've grown exhausted with it. You've seen it once. Imagine watching it for all eternity. Even as I write these words, a sly, subtle voice whispers sweet nothings in my head. "Ben," the voice calls, "Maybe this book will make you famous. Ben, maybe one day you'll be reciting these words before an enraptured crowd, every one of them clutching your book to their chests, hanging on your every word. It could happen, Ben. Just keep writing . . . just keep writing . . . any day now . . ."

For nearly forty years, I have struggled with ambition addiction, making momentous strides forward and then falling off the wagon, again and again. Why trust a sponsor in the midst of recovery, a guide such as myself who continues to struggle? First, I know the territory. I know the signs. I can help you identify ambition addiction, even as it hides insidiously behind a guise of cherished achievements. Second, while I may continue to struggle, while I still hear that sirens' song, I've made progress. *I've grown.* Life looks and feels a lot different today than it did before I began the recovery process. My approach to career, family, success, and failure has changed. My wife has noticed these positive developments. My children, too. My family and friends tell me I seem happier now, more at home in my skin and more at peace in my world. I'm still an ambition addict. A destructive strain of ambition still courses through my veins. That may never change. But I'm on the road to recovery. And it's working.

I offer myself as a mentor for another reason, too. While ambition addiction may manifest as tangible, concrete behavior, it is, fundamentally, an affliction of the soul. To free ourselves from destructive patterns, to live with integrity, and to find true happiness, we ambition addicts must engage the spirit. We must explore our relationship with divinity itself, whether we call that divinity God, Buddha, Allah, Brahma, Jesus, Atman, the Universe, the Force, Eternal Truth, a Higher Power, or the Interconnectedness of All Things. To turn from *Any Day Now* to this very real, very mortal moment, to open the door and, God help us, leave it open for good, takes courage, insight, and faith. As a spiritual guide and teacher, as a long-standing student of Eastern and Western wisdom traditions, as an ordained rabbi who has studied scripture in Jerusalem, meditated with monks in Tibet, stretched with yogis in India, and learned with spiritual masters far and wide, I can share the wise words and tried techniques that have helped me disconnect from *Any Day Now* and reconnect with my soul. I can point the way home.[3]

I am an ambition addict. I've learned how to diagnose this illness. I've navigated the twists and turns on the road to recovery. I can help you open the door. Whether or not you believe it, I'm your brother. We've tumbled into this hole together. Now, together, let's find the way out.

PART I

Ambition Addiction

Making a Diagnosis

Each of us has ambition. Our ambition may involve a healthy balance of hunger and humility, perseverance and perspective. On the other hand, perhaps without our even realizing it, our ambition may have soured. We may be, at this very moment, drifting further and further into full-scale ambition addiction, desperately grasping for our *Any Day Now* at the expense of our own and others' well-being. How would we know the difference? How can we determine whether ambition lifts us up or holds us down? How do we detect ambition addiction?

Before we launch into a formal diagnostic, it may help, at this point, to compare the following list of attributes with our own thoughts, feelings, and behaviors. Do any of these ambition addiction signs and symptoms resonate? Do we recognize any, or many, of these perspectives and behaviors in ourselves?

Following are ten signs and symptoms of ambition addiction:

- **Grandiose Dreams of All-Encompassing Glory:** We ambition addicts harbor detailed fantasies of the wondrous, happy endings toward which we strive. In these imagined happy endings, in our *Any Day Now*, we picture ourselves enjoying life free from insecurity, vulnerability, heartache, and fear. Such scenarios presuppose our dominance over others; by achieving astronomic accomplishments, fame, fortune, power, or prowess, we place ourselves, in our mind's eye, above the masses. We transcend, in our fantasies, the difficulties and doldrums of the human condition.

- **Contempt for the Present and Reverence for the Future:** Ambition addicts look to the future for salvation. Present reality, colored by shades of gray, full of tempestuous turmoil, forever in flux and ultimately untamable, can never and will never measure up to the fixed, fantastical future depicted by *Any Day Now*. As such, we ambition addicts view the present moment as a waiting room to endure, as one more hoop to jump through. Assessing the present moment with disappointment, discouragement, and even contempt, we frequently dissociate and disengage from activities and interactions throughout our day. Before an activity or interaction has even begun, we're looking down the pike, fixing our eyes on what's to come.
- **Single-Minded Focus on Goals and Objectives:** Ambition addicts treat current activities as necessary means to glorified ends. We may, at times, dive into projects, tasks, and to-do lists with feverish energy and excitement. We may appear passionately possessed, consumed by professional or personal activities and relationships. Nevertheless, we are primarily interested in the outcome of an activity or in the impact of a relationship, rather than in the activity or relationship itself.
- **Manic Pace:** In a choice between easy does it or fast and furious, ambition addicts will always choose fast and furious. Life begins, for us, only after we've reached our *Any Day Now*, an *Any Day Now* that could, at any moment, drift from sight and isappear. Consequently, we're forever in a rush, frequently ort on time, impatient with others, resentful of distractions impediments, and always very, *very* busy.

ety and Panic: Ambition addicts have dedicated their lives ltimately impossible undertaking. We don't simply want to win the prize. We don't merely hope to rise to the stars. We yearn to free ourselves from insecurity, vulnerability, and mortality. When life presents us with loose ends, confusion, frailties, fallibility, embarrassment, sadness, sickness, and death, we ambition addicts grow anxious. When no amount of subsequent striving or struggle enables us to outpace our incontrovertible humanity, we become neurotic and panicked. We see demons around every corner. We imagine disaster at every turn. We live in fear.

- **Severity and Depression:** Becoming number one is serious business! We ambition addicts understand that, unlike the plebeian proletariat in our midst, we have little time for inconsequential banter or lighthearted frivolity. *Any Day Now* could slip through our fingers at any moment; the stakes have never been higher. Consequently, we tackle each day with seriousness and severity. Perpetually dissatisfied, frequently resentful, we greet the world with gritted teeth and a furrowed brow. While the occasional victory may elevate our mood and lighten our disposition, we all too soon descend, when the high wears off, into disappointment, disillusionment, doom, and gloom.
- **Entitlement and Jealousy:** Ambition addicts equate *Any Day Now* with destiny. We believe our dreams have surfaced for good reason—they are not manifestations of unresolved trauma, but are rather the winds of fate lifting us toward a rightful, deserved, and inevitable future. We act, then, with a sense of justified bravado, boldly asserting our agendas and expecting others to capitulate and kowtow. We feel entitled to victory and gain; naturally, then, others must fall by the wayside to make room for our preeminence. When the opposite occurs, when others rise high and we feel left behind, we can be consumed by jealousy. We may view our own lives with contempt, disparaging whatever gains we've previously made and discounting whatever blessings we currently enjoy.

- **Distaste for Stasis and Equilibrium:** Though ambition addicts fear insecurity and vulnerability, we nevertheless hunger for forward movement and momentum. Change, in the form of personal and professional developments, reassures us that we are moving ever closer to our *Any Day Now*. Stress, in the form of high-stakes scenarios and high-intensity activities, exhilarates us; we find comfort in the rush. By that same token, we find stasis and equilibrium threatening. When things get too quiet, when life feels too monotonous and mundane, we suffocate, desperate for some indication that our glorious enterprise continues to unfold. Consequently, we avoid people, places, and situations that appear too staid and sedate, too quiet and complacent.
- **Difficulty Relaxing and Enjoying Simple Pleasures:** Connected with our distaste for stability and stasis, and connected also with our penchant for severity and speed, we ambition addicts have a hard time relaxing. Unscheduled hours make us nervous. Open-ended days, waiting periods, vacations, and sabbaticals fill us with dread, at least until we've discovered ways to use the time productively, or until we've enlisted the aid of alcohol, drugs, or pharmaceuticals. In similar fashion, ambition addicts find it challenging to enjoy simple activities and pleasures. We crave drama and excitement. We hunger for significance and substance. Meaningless recreation tends to bore us. If we must unwind, many of us prefer to do so through competitive activities or productive, quantifiable hobbies. Ambition *is* enjoyment. It's our path to delight. It's our drug of choice.
- **Categorical and Calculating Opinions of Others:** To actualize our dreams, we ambition addicts need others. We quickly and assiduously ascertain who, among our family members, friends, neighbors, community members, and colleagues, can help us achieve our goals. We lavish these individuals with our time and attention. We prioritize interactions with these individuals over

> interactions with those we deem peripheral to our progress. To these less advantageous individuals, to those we may love and adore yet who remain extraneous to our ambition, we scrupulously dole out our time, ever mindful that moments spent with "nonessentials" are moments we could otherwise spend reaching for the stars.

After reading this list of signs and symptoms, some of us may conclude that few, if any, of these qualities apply. We do not see our inner experience nor our outward behavior reflected in the vast majority of these descriptions. Of course, we could benefit from slowing down from time to time. Yeah, we might have trouble relaxing after a hectic and harried day. We don't, however, fit the bill of an ambition addict, not according to the depiction above. We're pretty sure we know some folks who do suffer from this addiction, and we've got a mind to slip this book under their door in the hopes it'll help them mend their ways; still, this isn't us. Ambition addiction is not our burden. We can breathe a sigh of relief.

Some of us, on the other hand, may have felt the hair rise on the back of our necks while reading this list of signs and symptoms. We have the uncanny sensation that we've been discovered, that our inner existence has been laid bare before us, our secret self a figurative and literal open book. We may not have dubbed our dreams with such cinematic terminology; yet, having ruminated on this phrase, *Any Day Now*, for some pages now, the title fits as well as any. Not to mention the fact that we do focus on the future, we do resent the success of others, we do avoid stasis and stability, and we do divide the world based on who might get us ahead. Like it or not, ambition addiction fits.

Whether we've concluded that ambition addiction does or does not apply to us, whether or not we feel saddled by this syndrome, I would recommend that we continue reading, at least for a few more pages. What follows is a step-by-step diagnostic, a relatively quick and easy exercise to help anyone determine if they do, or do not, suffer from ambition addiction. For many of us, this diagnostic will confirm what we've already concluded, and will do so while providing us, addicts and nonaddicts alike, with a valuable framework for assessing our ambition. For some of us, however, this diagnostic may reverse our conclusions, relieving our suspicions or alerting us to our addiction. Either way, we will, through the following diagnostic, benefit from a deeper look at our ambition, motivation, hopes, and dreams.

All addictive behaviors, from alcoholism to workaholism to ambition addiction, have two common traits: addictive behaviors are *persistent* and *counterproductive*. A gambling addict doesn't lose ten bucks every few weeks on the slots. A gambling addict gambles persistently and counterproductively. She remains glued to the craps table all night, misses work the following morning, and, bleary-eyed, buys more chips on her credit card. A nicotine addict doesn't lace a Saturday night buzz with a few cigarettes outside the bar. A nicotine addict smokes persistently and counterproductively, running sandpaper through his bronchioles and carpet bombing his alveoli morning, noon, and night.

To diagnose most addictions, then, we can zero in on a specific behavior, such as gambling or smoking, and ask: Is this behavior persistent and counterproductive? If the answer is yes, we've identified our addiction. With ambition addiction, however, identifying questionable behavior proves far more complex. Ambition addicts channel ambition into all sorts of activities. We ambitiously buy, sell, paint, parent, meditate, minister, write, date, or diet. Joe-the-ambition-addict may obsess over professional achievements while completely ignoring physical appearance. Jane-the-ambition-addict might care little about work yet will lift, tuck, and tighten her body with obsessive devotion. While most gambling addicts gamble, and most nicotine addicts smoke, when it comes to ambition addicts, no two individuals look alike.

To determine if we do, in fact, suffer from ambition addiction, we first need to identify our own unique set of ambition-infused behaviors. We need a detailed accounting of all behaviors into which we funnel our drive to succeed. Do we bring a spirit of striving to our professional lives, our personal relationships, or our physical appearance? Or perhaps all three?

We may find it helpful, at this point, to draw up a chart, listing ambitious behaviors on one side of the chart and less goal-oriented behaviors on the other. After filling in the chart, it might look something like this:

Table 1

	Easygoing Behavior *(Less goal-oriented)*	**Ambitious Behavior** *(Big hopes and dreams)*
Professional Life		Consulting work Book project
Personal Relationships	Relationship with wife Hanging out with friends	Relationship with daughters
Health and Appearance	Weekend soccer league	Weight lifting at the gym

In this example, our subject—let's call him Al—divides his behaviors into three categories (listed in the left-hand column): Professional Life, Personal Relationships, and Health and Appearance. When we construct our own chart (you can download chart templates and other helpful resources from my website, www.benjaminshalva.com), we can use these same categories, or we can add or substitute different categories such as: Hobbies, Volunteer Work, Social Activism, Religious and Spiritual Life, or Intellectual Pursuits.

Within the three categories Al has chosen, he lists seven behaviors: three easygoing, less goal-oriented behaviors in the center column, and four ambitious behaviors in the right-hand column. These seven behaviors don't compose the entirety of Al's existence, of course. He leaves out day-to-day activities such as "brushing teeth" or "buying groceries." He also excludes intermittent behaviors, such as "visiting Mom in Florida" and "annual consulting conference." The seven activities Al does include in his chart are the activities that take up most of his energy most of the time. These activities are his physical, emotional, intellectual, and spiritual bread and butter.

Notice that Al also leaves one box blank—the box corresponding to easygoing behaviors in his professional life. Al doesn't approach any aspect of his career in an easygoing manner. Whether answering e-mails, speaking with clients, or composing the latest chapter of his book, Al approaches the entirety of his professional life with an eye toward advancement. When making his chart, then, he leaves this box blank, labeling all of his professional endeavors as ambitious. As we complete our own charts, we, too, may find that a number of boxes remain blank. Certain categories of behavior will be dominated by an ambitious spirit. Other categories may involve little or no ambition at all. The key is not to fill in every box. The key is to list the major activities, ambitious or not, into which we direct the majority of our energy and attention.

Once we've divided our behaviors into easygoing behaviors and ambitious behaviors, we can proceed to step two of our diagnostic. Looking only at our ambitious behaviors, at those listed in the right-hand column of our charts, we hold each one under the microscope and ask: Do I perform this ambitious behavior *persistently*? When I ambitiously buy, sell, paint, parent, meditate, minister, date, or diet, do I do so occasionally or frequently? If one aspires to write the great American novel, if one imagines oneself posthumously enshrined as a twenty-first-century literary god, does one translate this ambition into irregularly scheduled writing sessions, tapping the keyboard for an hour every few weeks? Or does one write on a regular basis, utilizing a significant portion of one's time and energy to reach the stars?

Returning to Al's chart, we recall that he's identified four different ambitious behaviors—consulting work, a book project, his relationship with his daughters, and weight lifting at the gym. Al now asks himself: Which of these four ambitious behaviors do I engage in persistently? Regarding the first of these four behaviors, consulting work, Al admits to spending days, nights, and weekends at the office. He keeps a toothbrush in a desk drawer and a blanket and pillow near his office couch. When he happens to make it home, he steps away from family dinners to answer phone calls from his boss and composes work-related e-mails late into the night. Even on vacation, he keeps his smartphone close, knocking off items on his to-do list while his kids and wife splash in the pool. Yes indeed, Al's consulting work qualifies as persistent behavior.

Al moves on to his next ambitious behavior: his book project. Though he hates to admit it, Al's writing always seems to fall through the cracks. He wants a bestseller, but every time he sits down to write, he gets interrupted. He goes for long periods without writing at all, kicking himself for his inconsistency, yet, time and time again, finding reasons to put the writing on hold. So, unlike his consulting work, Al's writing does not qualify as persistent.

Al continues this process with each of his ambitious behaviors, identifying each one that he performs persistently. When finished, he highlights these persistent, ambitious behaviors on his chart:

Table 1A

	Easygoing Behavior *(Less goal-oriented)*	**Ambitious Behavior** *(Big hopes and dreams)*
Professional Life		Consulting work Book project
Personal Relationships	Relationship with wife Hanging out with friends	Relationship with daughters
Health and Appearance	Weekend soccer league	Weight Lifting at the gym

Once we've conducted this exercise ourselves, identifying all ambitious behaviors we perform persistently, we can move to step three. Looking at our persistently ambitious behaviors, we isolate each and ask: Is this persistent, ambitious behavior *counterproductive*? When I persistently and ambitiously buy, sell, paint, parent, meditate, minister, date, or diet, does my behavior hurt more than help? When I reach for the stars, do I elevate my own and others' lives, or do I create suffering within and without?

Diving into the moral minutiae of our persistently ambitious behavior propels us into murky waters. Is a given behavior counterproductive? That all depends. What appears productive to me may seem counterproductive to you. What you consider helpful, I may deem harmful. Rather than call the whole thing off, individuals who are morally mature and emotionally grounded muddle through such ambiguity. They behave ambitiously, observe the outcomes, reflect on the relative happiness and suffering created, and, if needed, adjust their behavior. They buffer best guesses with hope and humility. They remain open to feedback from family, friends, colleagues, and community. Such individuals understand that morality is as much art as science. They may not always get it right, but they try their best to act with compassion and care.

Not so for ambition addicts. At the first hint of pain, pain we've inflicted upon ourselves or pain we've caused another, we tend to hide. We flee from reality's bright lights to *Any Day Now*'s darkened theater. We self-soothe through dissociation and fantasy, answering any lingering doubts with platitudes like "to make an omelette, you've gotta break some eggs."

The more we employ this escape route, the less practiced we become at navigating complex moral terrain. *Any Day Now* keeps us locked into prefab patterns of behavior, behavior designed to get us what we want regardless of the repercussions. Ruthless ambition becomes our only compass, our one true north. Our eyes see only stars. Our ears hear only applause. Our facility for self-reflection erodes, preventing us from honestly assessing our behavior and making any needed adjustments.

To determine if we suffer from ambition addiction, we need to answer the question: Is our persistent, ambitious behavior counterproductive? However, if we do, in fact, suffer from ambition addiction, our addiction prevents us from accurately answering this question. Under the spell of *Any Day Now*, we may lack the facility for self-reflection. Yet, self-reflection is exactly what we need to make a diagnosis. We've run into a diagnostic catch-22.

To sidestep this predicament, we can approach the issue of counterproductive behavior from a slightly different direction. Rather than ask, "Are my behaviors counterproductive?" we can ask, "Are my *goals* counterproductive?" When I buy, sell, paint, parent, meditate, minister, date, or diet, do I reach for goals that take into account the physical, emotional, intellectual, and spiritual well-being of myself and others? Or, do I dream counterproductive dreams, aiming for goals that disregard my own and others' welfare? Rather than assess the impact of our actions, we can identify counterproductive behavior by examining our motivations. We can ask one simple question: *What do I want?*

The road to hell is not paved with good intentions. The road to hell is paved with unexamined intentions. All ambitious behavior, productive or counterproductive, healthy or addictive, stems from this fundamental question: *What do I want?* When we strive for productive goals, goals that take into consideration the health and happiness of ourselves and others, these productive goals guide us toward productive behavior. Whether or not we succeed in our ambitious efforts, we will have reached for our objectives with the right intention, maximizing benefit, minimizing harm. When we strive for counterproductive goals, on the other hand, goals that prioritize egoistic glory over compassionate concern, goals built on a foundation of fear, insecurity, anger, and self-loathing, these goals guide our actions as well. Minute by minute, day by day, we transform counterproductive intentions into destructive behavior, sacrificing the greater good for our triumph and glory.

The question *"What do I want?"* acts as a prism, refracting individual behaviors into a spectrum of desire. We may perform a given ambitious behavior for a variety of reasons. Behind some ambitious conduct, we may discover an alchemy of altruism and ego. At this point in our diagnostic process, we note every goal, no matter how virtuous, unscrupulous, sensible, or absurd. Successfully identifying ambition addiction hinges on this detailed accounting of desire.

Returning to our previous chart (Table 1A), Al previously highlighted three persistent, ambitious behaviors—consulting work, relationship with daughters, and weight-lifting sessions at the gym. For Al to determine if he does, in fact, suffer from ambition addiction, he now shines the spotlight on these three highlighted behaviors and asks of each: *What do I want?*

Al wants a lot of things. He wants to take over his consulting firm and retire with billions. He wants the world as his golf course and his kids' trust funds overflowing. He wants his three little girls to blossom into three wonderfully accomplished, beautiful women, mothers to his grandchildren, blessings to his name. Despite his late-night visits to the fridge and frequent detours to the drive-thru, Al wants to see his hundredth birthday. He also wouldn't mind looking in the mirror after a session at the gym and seeing a shirtless, sculpted Matthew McConaughey looking back. Any day now, Al would love to walk down the street and make women swoon.

Adding a new column to his chart, Al completes step three by recording each of these goals next to their corresponding behaviors:

Table 1B

	Easygoing Behavior ***(Less goal-oriented)***	**Ambitious Behavior** ***(Big hopes and dreams)***	**Goals** ***(What do I want?)***
Professional Life		Consulting work Book project	*Consulting Goal #1*: **I want to take over the company and retire with billions.** *Consulting Goal #2*: **I want to leave an ample trust fund for my daughters.**

	Easygoing Behavior *(Less goal-oriented)*	Ambitious Behavior *(Big hopes and dreams)*	Goals *(What do I want?)*
Personal Relationships	Relationship with wife Hanging out with friends	Relationship with daughters	*Fatherhood Goal #1*: **I want my daughters to grow up into amazing women and mothers.**
Health and Appearance	Weekend soccer league	Weight lifting at the gym	*Weight-Lifting Goal #1*: **I want a healthy body.** *Weight-Lifting Goal #2*: **I want to look like Matthew McConaughey and make women swoon.**

Now, the moment of truth. Al must determine if any of his goals aggrandize the ego at the expense of his own or others' well-being. Al needs to identify goals that suck the air from the room, suffocating colleagues, family, friends, and himself alike. Such counterproductive goals will inevitably point him toward counterproductive behavior. And counterproductive behavior, performed persistently and ambitiously, is a clear indication that Al has succumbed to ambition addiction.

Al begins this final step in our diagnostic by taking a look at the goals concerning his daughters' financial and emotional well-being:

> *I want to leave an ample trust fund for my daughters (Consulting Goal #2).*

> *I want my daughters to grow up into amazing women and mothers (Fatherhood Goal #1).*

Al can see that his parental gratification doesn't hinge on anyone else's defeat. These goals don't require him to hide behind the wings at beauty pageants, ferociously screaming at his little angels and cutting holes in competitors' tutus. Al doesn't need his daughters to be the best.

He just wants them to be happy and healthy. He'd like them to have some money in the bank to keep them afloat. Al's girls mean the world to him, but the world doesn't revolve around his girls. The verdict: *I want to leave an ample trust fund for my daughters (Consulting Goal #2)* and *I want my daughters to grow up into amazing women and mothers (Fatherhood Goal #1)* do not qualify as counterproductive.

Next, Al takes a look at the first of his weight-lifting goals:

I want a healthy body (Weight-Lifting Goal #1).

Al wants to blow out the candles on his one-hundredth birthday, but not at the expense of others' health and well-being. Al wants to feel good, but his happiness doesn't require anyone else to suffer. If anything, all those curls at the gym will help him lift his future grandkids. Everybody wins. *I want a healthy body (Weight-Lifting Goal #1)* does not qualify as counterproductive.

Al then turns to the two remaining goals on his chart (cue ominous music):

I want to take over the company and retire with billions (Consulting Goal #1).

I want to look like Matthew McConaughey and make women swoon (Weight-Lifting Goal #2).

Al saves these two goals for last, suspecting that one or both might qualify as unhealthy and counterproductive. These goals shimmer like sports cars on a showroom floor, quickening the pulse, intoxicating the senses: beautiful, breathtaking, dangerous. When Al dreams these dreams, his eyes glaze over. Goose bumps run up and down his arms. He salivates and thinks to himself, "It could happen . . . any day now . . ."

Based on this reaction alone, Al wonders if he's discovered two goals that qualify as counterproductive. Still, he's not sure. Counterproductive goals elevate the ego at the expense of one's own and others' health and happiness. At first glance, the goal *I want to take over the company and retire with billions* fits this description. To take over the company, Al will need to take down the competition—fellow CEOs-to-be Tom, Dick, and Harry. Al will also need to all but abandon his wife, Val (yep, that's right, Al married Val), spending nights and weekends at the office and sequestering any free hours for his daughters, the apples of his eye. Seizing the corporate throne will require a great deal of sacrifice. Enemies will be made. Heads will roll. A lonely wife will drink alone.

Still, Al hesitates. "This is ridiculous," he thinks. "Yes, I want to win. Yes, to get what I want, my colleagues and my family will suffer. But the end more than justifies the means. When I take over the firm, my family will never want for money again. My wife, my children, my future grandkids—their happiness will increase right along with mine. Is that selfish? Is that counterproductive? Becoming CEO is for them, too."

Many of us, like Al, point to imagined happy endings to justify potentially unhealthy goals. Dreaming the impossible dream causes some suffering, sure. But this suffering paves the way for an *Any Day Now* of unparalleled bliss. Don't productive ends justify counterproductive means?

If, during this diagnostic exercise, we find ourselves in such a quandary, unable to decide if a goal helps or harms, unsure whether imagined ends justify injurious means, we can ask the following question:

Is my goal an all-or-nothing goal?

All-or-nothing goals allow no room for second place. We don't just want a profitable business. We want a monopoly. We don't just want a happy, healthy, well-educated child. We want a Harvard valedictorian. A winning season is not enough. Until we've won that Super Bowl ring, we can't relax. We can't exhale and enjoy.

By leaving no room for second place, for good enough, for shades of gray, all-or-nothing goals can create a great deal of collateral damage.

The pressure created by all-or-nothing goals wreaks havoc on our physical health, our personal and professional relationships, and our spiritual well-being. By setting our sights on the stratosphere, we leave no available energy for body, heart, and soul. We also allow little time for professional or personal relationships that don't directly serve our all-or-nothing interests.

Yet, just like Al, many of us justify this collateral damage with the promise of a happy ending. Once we've monopolized the industry, we think, our family will never worry about money again. Once our golden child graduates from Harvard, she will have all she needs to navigate this harsh, cruel world. All-or-nothing goals beckon like a mirage, a promise of soft shade. We imagine our *Any Day Now* will bring us relief from the toil and tumult of being human. To arrive at such bliss, we'll do just about anything.

On the day after we win the election, the Super Bowl, the Oscar, that's when we see this mirage for what it truly is—sand running through our fingers, merely a trick of the light. We've won our all-or-nothing prize, but now even more people have come knocking at our door, demanding our time and attention. If we don't want to tumble back down the mountain, if we don't want our newfound status and power to crumble, we will have to work even harder than before. Our all-or-nothing goal has proven itself a some-or-nothing goal. A new mirage hovers, distant, beyond the dunes. Here we go again, crawling beneath that blistering sun.

As one intimately familiar with all-or-nothing goals, as one who has struggled toward one mirage after another, I can testify that *all-or-nothing goals do not bring happiness*. That big win won't make everything better, not for ourselves and not for the ones we love. The first time I glimpsed all-or-nothing's illusory nature came in my early twenties, when my brother, Joel, and I attended a Shakespeare in the Park production of Chekov's *The Seagull*. The cast included Meryl Streep, Kevin Kline, Christopher Walken, Natalie Portman, Marcia Gay Harden, Philip Seymour Hoffman, and John Goodman. And on this night, the final night of the run, countless stars of stage and screen filled Central Park's open-air Delacorte Theater. Joel and I found our seats a few rows behind Dustin Hoffman and directly in front of Carol Kane, her delightful cackle of a voice complaining about the upcoming pilot season. I felt like I'd entered the pages of *People* magazine. Everywhere I looked, stars shone bright.

Our tickets allowed us entry to *The Seagull*'s after party, a paparazzi-assaulted affair at the Russian Tea Room. As if in a dream, I stumbled down the red carpet outside that legendary venue, photographers lowering their lenses and muttering, "Who is that? Oh, that's no one." I, the no one in reference, spent the rest of the evening nervously hobnobbing with multimillionaire movie stars and calming my nerves with shots of chilled vodka poured down a giant luge of ice.

At one point, while waiting in line for hors d'oeuvres, I heard someone yell, "Caviar crepes!" Suddenly, a herd of Hollywood's elite scampered into line behind me. Sure enough, a caterer had produced a metal tray filled with caviar-stuffed crepes. The line surged forward, bodies pressing against my back. It looked, for a moment, like the person in front of me had taken the last two crepes. Groans and complaints erupted from the crowd. A caterer rushed out with a fresh batch. Squeals of delight.

That evening, I tasted life at the top. I met stars who'd gambled on all-or-nothing goals and won big. Yet, here they were, bouncing up and down for crepes. The red carpet, the flashing cameras, all that fame and fortune didn't matter. The fact that many in that line could afford their own caviar-stuffed delicacies served to them on a silver tray by a private chef morning, noon, and night didn't matter. These celebrities' all-or-nothing mirages had failed to quench their thirst. All that fame, all that fortune; still, they wandered the world with hungry eyes.

When we justify all-or-nothing goals with promises of future happiness, we delude ourselves. All-or-nothing ambition is a ravaging fire, a fire upon which we grow dependent for heat and light. To keep it alive, we will continue to batter our bodies, hearts, and souls. We will continue to neglect our family and friends. Even if we cash in some big winnings, even if we offer reparations to those we've abandoned, the people we love will continue to suffer. That wunderkind at Harvard—all he ever wanted was our time and attention. That jewel-adorned spouse—she now drinks the finest wine money can buy. But, per usual, she drinks it alone.

Forced to admit that *I want to take over the company and retire with billions (Consulting Goal #1)* qualifies as an all-or-nothing goal, Al highlights this goal in his chart:

Table 1C

	Easygoing Behavior ***(Less goal-oriented)***	**Ambitious Behavior** ***(Big hopes and dreams)***	**Goals** ***(What do I want?)***
Professional Life		Consulting work Book project	<u>*Consulting Goal #1:*</u> **I want to take over the company and retire with billions.** <u>*Consulting Goal #2:*</u> **I want to leave an ample trust fund for my daughters.**
Personal Relationships	Relationship with wife Hanging out with friends	Relationship with daughters	<u>*Fatherhood Goal #1:*</u> **I want my daughters to grow up into amazing women and mothers.**
Health and Appearance	Weekend soccer league	Weight lifting at the gym	<u>*Weight-Lifting Goal #1*</u>: **I want a healthy body.** <u>*Weight-Lifting Goal #2*</u>: **I want to look like Matthew McConaughey and make women swoon.**

Al then moves on to his final, unscrutinized goal:

I want to look like Matthew McConaughey and make women swoon (Weight-Lifting Goal #2).

Again, Al's not sure what to do. On the one hand, this goal feels a little selfish. It benefits Al and Al alone. On the other hand, a counterproductive goal isn't simply a selfish goal. It's a goal that hurts more than helps. Counterproductive goals create suffering. Does anyone suffer from Al's red-faced, vein-popping visits to the gym? Even if, any day now, he looks in the mirror and sees Matthew McConaughey staring back, even if his dashing physique makes women weak in the knees, what's the big deal? He's not planning on bedding this cadre of admirers. He just wants a little ego stroking. No harm, no foul, right?

We may find ourselves in a similar conundrum, scrutinizing what seems like a slightly selfish, admittedly egocentric goal and wondering, "What's the harm?" So we want some attention, some money, a little power and glory—big deal. We're not committing corporate fraud or clubbing baby seals. Can't we allow ourselves this bit of benign indulgence?

To determine if an apparently harmless goal qualifies as counterproductive, we can ask ourselves another clarifying question:

Does my goal objectify myself or others?

Goals that objectify oneself or others naturally ripen into counterproductive behavior. When we view ourselves and others as shallow, two-dimensional objects, we feel justified in manipulating these objects to get what we want. We disregard the physical, emotional, and spiritual repercussions of our manipulations, skimming the surface without a care for the deeper currents our actions generate. We see ourselves and others as tools, mere means to our coveted ends. This leads us to act with insensitivity, even cruelty, at times; indifferent to our own and others' suffering, we command and cajole, intimidate and machinate, unscrupulously attempting to conquer any and all resistance.

Al's goal—*I want to look like Matthew McConaughey and make women swoon*—objectifies himself and objectifies others. Al objectifies himself by conceiving of himself as a pre-Photoshopped, two-dimensional image, an image in need of some fine, or not so fine, tuning. He charges to the free weights with this image in mind, turning up his iPod and turning down the feedback from his body. He lifts, presses, and curls far beyond capacity. His heart strains. His tendons flare. His vertebrae groan and his disks start to slip. A vision of McConaughey in his mind's eye, Al inadvertently steamrolls over the very body he hopes to improve.

Al's goal also objectifies others. Exiting the gym, flushed from his last set of curls, he searches for a member of the opposite sex, hoping she'll swoon in his direction. In this moment, women exist solely to stroke Al's ego. When he passes one attractive woman climbing from her car, Al sees her in only two dimensions. In actuality, she is a complex human being, filled to the brim with thoughts and feelings, spirit and soul; however, in Al's mind, she's become, to quote Andrew Dice Clay, "two tits, a hole, and a heartbeat."[4] Al has little compunction eyeing her up and down and giving a little wink. He pays no mind to her furrowed brow, the way she dodges his leer and speeds her stride. Al wouldn't know this, but he's the fifth guy today who's eyed her like a piece of meat. He's the fifth guy today who's turned her world into shark-infested waters. As she walks away, emotionally exhausted, spiritually spent, Al climbs into his car and thinks, "Man, I love the gym."

Recognizing that his goal—*I want to look like Matthew McConaughey and make women swoon (Weight-Lifting Goal #2)*—objectifies himself and others, Al highlights this goal on his chart as well:

TABLE 1D

	Easygoing Behavior ***(Less goal-oriented)***	**Ambitious Behavior** ***(Big hopes and dreams)***	**Goals** ***(What do I want?)***
Professional Life		Consulting work Book project	*Consulting Goal #1:* **I want to take over the company and retire with billions.** *Consulting Goal #2:* **I want to leave an ample trust fund for my daughters.**
Personal Relationships	Relationship with wife Hanging out with friends	Relationship with daughters	*Fatherhood Goal #1:* **I want my daughters to grow up into amazing women and mothers.**
Health and Appearance	Weekend soccer league	Weight lifting at the gym	*Weight-Lifting Goal #1:* **I want a healthy body.** *Weight Lifting Goal #2:* **I want to look like Matthew McConaughey and make women swoon.**

Now that Al has highlighted two counterproductive goals—one goal that drives his consulting work and one goal that fuels his weight-lifting sessions—he can safely assume these two behaviors, consulting and lifting, qualify as counterproductive. Al is dying, just dying, to be a CEO with a *GQ* physique. To realize his *Any Day Now*, to get what he wants, he will intentionally or unintentionally harm his colleagues, his wife, his daughters, himself, and even unwitting passersby in the gym parking lot. His ambition in these arenas feeds his ego at the expense of health, happiness, and well-being.

Al has received his diagnosis. His ambitious behavior, at work and at the gym, is persistent and counterproductive. He is an ambition addict.

As we complete this final step ourselves, we may find that each of our persistent, ambitious behaviors stem from productive, healthy goals—goals that respect our own and others' well-being, goals that boost us up without denigrating others. If this is the case, our test has come back negative. We may aspire to great heights. We may hunger for monumental achievements. Nevertheless, we've managed to stoke ambition's fire without allowing it to blaze out of control. We may be ambitious, intensely ambitious, even, but we are not ambition addicts.

If, on the other hand, any of our persistent, ambitious behaviors stem from counterproductive goals—all-or-nothing goals, goals that objectify, goals that hurt more than help, goals that create suffering for ourselves and our world—our test has come back positive. Whether or not we feel it, regardless if we believe it, we have a problem. Our ambition has mutated into malignancy. *Any Day Now* runs the show. We've grown dependent on fantastical, all-or-nothing, surface-level, egocentric ambition to get through the day. Ambition owns us. We can't live without it. We are ambition addicts.

Those of us in the throes of addiction—addiction of any kind—will, if we're so blessed, arrive at such a moment of truth. Looking at ourselves with unabashed honesty, seeing our reflection in the tearful eyes of those we love, we will utter that most courageous and liberating declaration: "I have a problem." The instant we give voice to this secret suffering, our previously monolithic path cleaves in two. Where no choice existed, now we have a choice. In one direction, we see a wind-in-your-hair highway, a straight shot to *Any Day Now*. In the other direction, we see a thin, meandering trail winding its way into the wilderness, a path overrun with weeds and choked with fellow travelers. Where this second road leads, we don't know. We're not even sure we want to know.

Diagnosing our addiction places us right here—at a crossroads between certainty and mystery, between a predictable path and a wild expanse of moral ambiguity, emotional vulnerability, and no-bullshit mortality. The choice, for most of us, is anything but clear. Armed with our diagnosis, having named our addiction, we stand frozen at this crossroads. Where do we go from here? What road will we choose?

Dying to Win

From a distance, a star looks peaceful—a serene, tranquil jewel floating within the vast night sky. In reality, however, a star is an explosion, hydrogen shattering into helium, a blazing, forever-hungry fire. To achieve the all-encompassing win, to dominate the industry and dazzle the competition, to build a pyramid and to balance as Pharaoh atop its precarious point, ambition addicts require a tremendous amount of energy. Even if we addicts draw a portion of this energy from the willing and unwilling in our midst, the primary source of fuel needs to come from ourselves. We fill ambition's tank with our own bodies, hearts, and souls. Then we light a spark and explode.

"You must have a RAGE to succeed," explains lawyer-to-the-stars Larry A. Thompson in his book, *Shine: A Powerful 4-Step Plan for Becoming a Star in Anything You Do*. "You must have tunnel vision—a one-way ticket—do or die. You must have a mad passion for success."[5] "Tunnel vision," according to Thompson, involves an unequivocal investment of one's entire being, one's body, heart, and soul. To become a star, Thompson continues, we have to "want it, need it, breathe it, eat it, dream it, pray for it, work at it, sacrifice for it, beg for it, get it."[6] The entirety of our existence must point toward our goal.

Before we forge ahead on such an all-consuming journey, before we continue to invest such a tremendous amount of personal capital in our ambitious pursuits, we addicts would be wise to ask: Is it worth it? Is ambition addiction's prize worth ambition addiction's cost? If we continue to pursue our *Any Day Now,* how will this unfettered ambition affect us physically, emotionally, and spiritually? How might our "rage to succeed" impact our family, friends, colleagues, and communities? Standing at a crossroads between *Any Day Now* and the road to recovery, this cost-benefit analysis can help us choose which path to take.

We begin our analysis by focusing on ambition addiction's most tangible consequence—the gradual degradation of our physical body. Depending on the degree of our ambition, the rhythms of our lifestyle, and the designs of our DNA, ambition's fire could leave us imperceptibly weakened or dramatically debilitated. Some of us, for a good long while, can chase our *Any Day Now* without ill effect. Others will drop dead from a heart attack long before grabbing that brass ring. Most of us will fall somewhere in between. Ambition addiction won't kill us, but it will certainly leave its mark.

For addicts and nonaddicts alike, dramatic changes in one's environment trigger a chain reaction in one's body. This chain reaction, beginning with environmental flux and ending with physiological response, is called *stress.* Stress can occur even when we get what we want, even when we win. We may have wanted our situation to change. We may have visualized these changes. When these changes manifest, however, our minds may rejoice, but our bodies will still recoil. The body views any major shift in context, good or bad, as a threat. The most glorious of victories still triggers vigilance beneath our skin.[7]

Take, for example, an executive working at a high-powered advertising agency. One morning, her boss invites her out to lunch and tells her, between mouthfuls of salad, that she's been promoted.

"This new position will involve a lot of hard work," the boss warns. "You'll be managing two teams on two different coasts. You'll need to fly out to the West Coast a few times a month to coordinate with our San Francisco branch. And as deputy director, you'll present to our shareholders every quarter. So, you ready for this?"

Our hero smiles, a leaf of overdressed spinach dangling deftly from her fork. *Yes. Yes I am.* She's confident. She's ready. Together, boss and protégée toast over glasses of Pinot Grigio before finishing their lunch and sharing a cab back to the office.

That afternoon, at her desk, our ad exec sips a cup of coffee, swivels in her chair to face the window and the cityscape beyond, and replays the lunch meeting in her head. *You'll be managing two teams . . . You'll need to fly out to the West Coast a few times a month . . . You'll present to our shareholders . . . You ready for this?* As the words sink in, she realizes her whole world is about to change. Winning has launched her beyond her comfort zone. *Oy vey!*

This inaugural *Oy vey!*, this stress-filled blend of jubilance and terror, initiates a biochemical avalanche. First, our protagonist's limbic system, which includes portions of her cerebral cortex as well as deeper brain structures, flashes a simple message: *Threat! Threat! Threat!* The limbic system, also known more colorfully as the paleomammalian brain, lacks an appreciation for nuance. It fears change, pure and simple. Send it a terminal diagnosis or a long-desired promotion—it will sing the same tune: *Threat! Threat! Threat!*

As our hero continues to gaze out her office window, her limbic system sends this code red to another part of the brain—the hypothalamus. Ever the good soldier, the hypothalamus passes the message to the pituitary gland, which responds by secreting adrenocorticotropic hormone (ACTH). ACTH is a seasoned traveler. It quickly hitches a ride down the bloodstream until it reaches the adrenal glands, nested atop the kidneys. When these adrenals get a whiff of ACTH, they, in turn, whip up a batch of two more hormones, adrenaline and cortisol, and send these bosom buddies swimming into the bloodstream.[8]

From the outside, our executive may appear calm and collected, casually sipping her coffee, quietly contemplating her future. On the inside, however, the dynamic duo of cortisol and adrenaline have launched her into fight-or-flight. Her respiration rate, heart rate, and blood pressure have begun to soar. Her circulatory system has diverted the resulting high-speed, oxygenated blood away from her torso and into her arms and legs, preparing these limbs for battle.[9] Within nanoseconds, before she even realizes it, her body is ready for war.

Hopefully, after thirty minutes, or perhaps an hour or two, that initial *Oy vey!* will shift back to an *A-OK.* Our newly minted manager will take some deep breaths, turn to her work, and send out some e-mails. Her body will demilitarize, stabilizing her respiration rate, heart rate, and blood pressure. Regular blood flow will return to her torso, nourishing her digestive system and enabling her fluttering stomach to absorb the nutrients from lunch. Nerve receptors and enzymes will lasso adrenaline and cortisol and give these troublemakers the heave-ho. As our hero comes to terms with her shifting context, her body returns to its regularly scheduled program.

Unless she's an ambition addict. Unlike most individuals, ambition addicts perceive equilibrium, itself, as a threat. We've constructed our *Any Day Now* upon the premise that the present moment is not enough. Our dreams demand forward motion. Calm, quiet afternoons send us running for the hills. When life gets same-old and humdrum, we respond with a flurry of activity. *Ambition addicts seek stress.* The presence of perpetual fight-or-flight reassures us that we're on the move, one leap closer to our *Any Day Now.*

As we addicts turn our limbic system's sporadic alarm into a steady mantra, as we consciously and consistently place ourselves in situations that elicit fight-or-flight, our body responds by secreting a steady stream of adrenaline and cortisol. What began as a temporary and benign increase in blood pressure, triggered by a momentary influx of hormones, starts to transform into chronic high blood pressure, aka hypertension. Hypertension increases our risk for atherosclerosis, a thickening of the arterial walls that prevents sufficient blood from reaching vital organs. Our heart cells, deprived of the oxygen and nutrients they need, begin to die. Our brain cells begin to die. We may be getting closer to our *Any Day Now*. We may also be edging closer to a heart attack or stroke.[10]

To add insult to injury, hypertension, caused by constant fight-or-flight, can also narrow the arteries that feed our kidneys. As less and less blood reaches our kidneys, the blood pressure within the kidneys decreases. The kidneys then compensate, secreting hormones aimed to raise our blood pressure. The worse the hypertension, the worse the atherosclerosis. The worse the atherosclerosis, the more our kidneys work to elevate our blood pressure even further, bringing us closer still to coronary and cerebral malfunction.[11]

In addition to raising our blood pressure and contributing to coronary and cerebral degradation, a perpetual fight-or-flight response also debilitates our immune system, aggravates our digestive system, and dangerously increases our cells' production of free radicals. This multitargeted assault leads to a laundry list of additional health problems, including immune system impairment, inflammation, premature aging, thinning of the cerebral cortex, irritable bowel syndrome, reflux, and asthma.[12] While our bodies can tolerate the occasional, or even not so occasional *Oy vey!* reaction, chronic stress erodes our strength, impairs our health, and brings us ever closer to full physiological collapse.

Yet, as fight-or-flight becomes our new normal, many addicts grow anesthetized to even the most conspicuous symptoms of stress.[13] We get used to navigating our lives with a pounding heart, a tense stomach, and tight shoulders. What years ago felt like overwhelming panic now feels like a typical Tuesday spent reaching for the stars. Over time, however, as this steady diet of stress pummels us from within, our body begins to succumb. Organs fail. Systems shut down. The body can fight no longer. The end draws near.

Such was the case for the voraciously ambitious Bill Parcells, the famed professional football coach who won two Super Bowls with the New York Giants in the 1986/87 and 1990/91 seasons. On the outside, Parcells was a star, a cantankerous captain whose ambition earned him trophies, notoriety, respect, admiration, and millions of dollars. On the inside, however, his body was falling apart.

Professional football coaches, by definition, are a stressed-out lot. Brian Billick, the coach of the Baltimore Ravens from 1999 to 2007, describes the life of an NFL coach this way:

> You spend massive amounts of time away from your family, you push yourself to extreme exhaustion and beyond—the drug of choice among most football coaches is Diet Coke, consumed in copious amounts—and you compete in an unforgiving forum, with a rapt public hanging on the outcome of each game.[14]

Jim Schwartz, the head coach for the Detroit Lions from 2009 to 2013, adds, "Coaches don't work 100 hours a week because that's healthy. They do it because the job requires it. That's what it is. We're worried about getting the job done, getting wins on Sunday."[15]

This cocktail of enormous stress and taxing lifestyle has caused even run-of-the-mill coaches to clutch their chests and toss back the Tums. Bill Parcells, however, was no ordinary coach. No man has done what Parcells has done. No mortal has coached four different NFL teams to the playoffs. Four teams, I might add, who, before Parcells's arrival, suffered season after season of dismal defeats. Such miraculous feats brought Parcells fame, fortune, and permanent homage in the Pro Football Hall of Fame. His efforts earned him eternal life in the annals of sports history.

How did he do it? What fueled his meteoric rise? How did Parcells win? *Ambition.* Parcells's ambition woke him before the dawn. It kept him furious and hungry, his face, according to journalist Michael Lewis, "a study in dissatisfaction . . . as if he's eaten a bad oyster."[16] Even as a champion of champions, Parcells had this to say: "No matter how much you've won, no matter how many games, no matter how many championships, no matter how many Super Bowls, you're not winning now, so you stink."[17] This immutable hunger for the omnipresent win separated Parcells from the garden-variety coaches of his era. Parcells left it all out on the field.

The stress of chasing that Lombardi Trophy, season after season, decade after decade, nearly cost Parcells his life. The first system to go was his gut. In addition to raising one's blood pressure, stress hormones prepare the body for digestion by signaling the liver to fill the gallbladder with bile. The constant flood of stress hormones through Parcells's veins sent his liver and gallbladder into overdrive. Massive amounts of bile flooded his small intestine, where the bile boiled, bubbled, and, in the dead of night, spewed into his mouth, choking him awake on his own acidic brew.[18]

At the same time that his perpetual fight-or-flight wreaked havoc with his gut, it also contributed to Parcells's weight gain, high cholesterol, fainting spells, arrhythmia, and coronary artery disease. At the age of fifty-one, "Big Tuna," as his players affectionately called him, underwent three angioplasties followed by coronary bypass surgery, a surgery from which Parcells was not sure he would emerge alive.[19]

Thankfully for Parcells and his family, friends, and fans, he survived it all. Now in his seventies, he enjoys retirement and a part-time gig as a commentator on ESPN. Parcells gambled and won. He put his life on the line for his Super Bowl dreams and he lived to tell the tale.

Parcells was one of the lucky ones. His genetic predisposition, his physical fortitude, and his kick-ass team of top-of-the-line cardiologists kept him in the game. Will the rest of us ambition addicts be so lucky? How many of us will reach the finish line before our ever-narrowing arteries, our strangled heart, our suffocating brain, our shrunken kidneys, our kamikaze immune systems, and our irritable, bile-filled bowels sideline us for good?

Furthermore, even if Parcells had suddenly and tragically dropped dead on the sidelines from a heart attack or stroke, he would have died with Super Bowl rings on his fingers and flashbulbs in his eyes. The majority of us, of course, will never reach such heights nor enjoy such renown. We may spend the rest of our days struggling in obscurity and toiling in frustration, only to find ourselves abruptly, perhaps irrevocably, yanked from the game. Ambition addiction is a roll of the dice. To reach for the stars, we put our very lives on the line. Some of us, like Parcells, will feel the sting of the scalpel yet emerge victorious. Others will die trying.

Burning Bridges

Just as ambition addiction requires a sacrifice of body, ambition addiction requires a sacrifice of heart. To live as gods among men, ambition addicts must sequester the heart, lest its palpitations dampen ambition's fire. We addicts cannot allow love—debilitating, irrational, untamable love—to derail us from our dreams. We must make war, not love. Lovers don't win. Lovers end up locked down with a mortgage and rug rats, and we never hear from the suckers again.

Spouses, children, family, and friends, the individuals who love us for who we are, not for what we do, slow us down. They haven't subscribed to our *Any Day Now*. They don't appreciate the preeminence of our vision, the all-encompassing rage with which we tackle our dreams. The less time we allow in our schedules for family dinners and beers with the buds, the more our family and friends will likely voice their dissent. We used to be around more, they object. We used to be fun, they accuse. Rather than support our manifest destiny, they clamor for the good old days, the days when, stuck in a rut, we at least had time for someone other than ourselves.

If we opt for a lukewarm pool of love and fidelity over the blazing fire of ambition and conquest, we risk losing our edge. With every acquiescence, we more closely resemble those schlubs in the suburbs, dutifully tending to their mediocre lives. To reach for our *Any Day Now*, we have to protect ourselves against empathy and sentimentality.

We have to inoculate ourselves against guilt and shame. We must stop listening to the ones we love.

While muting the call of family and friends allows us to focus more exclusively on our *Any Day Now*, we may eventually need to go a step further. To shine like a star, we may need to permanently sever intimate relationships that stand in our way. Entrepreneur Michael Fulmore, in his book *Unleashing Your Ambition*, encourages this no-mercy approach:

> In some cases, burning bridges may be your only hope to the success you want. If the bridges you have only connect you to the opposite of what you want, then let them burn. Choose to walk away from the things and people you've outgrown.[20]

As we goose-step our way to greatness, as we outpace less ambitious family and friends, we may reach a turning point when we must cut the cord and walk away.

Bill Parcells knew how to cut the cord. On his hunt for a Super Bowl title, Parcells gave up on any semblance of work-life balance. He consistently chose meetings, practices, games, and beers at the bar over the doldrums of family life. His ambition addiction enabled him to turn down his daughter when she asked him to be her date for the elementary school dance. His tunnel vision enabled him to skip not one, not two, but all three of his daughters' college graduations. And when Parcells did happen to grace his own doorstep, rage kept him focused, brooding—a coaching machine even at the dinner table. "I don't think I was an overly warm parent," Parcells admits.[21]

Nor was Parcells an overly warm husband. He cheated early and often, leaving home for days at a time on what his family referred to as his "mystery vacations." Eventually, at age fifty-seven, Parcells began an affair with a married twenty-nine-year-old waitress at B. K. Sweeney's, his favorite watering hole. His wife, Judy, who'd held on through so many previous infidelities, finally filed for divorce. Bridge burned.[22]

One might argue that the life of an NFL coach demands this type of emotional indelicacy. Some might insist that anyone at the helm of a multimillion-dollar franchise has to prioritize work over other concerns. But Parcells, himself, disagrees. "It was always something at my job that kept me away, but it didn't keep other coaches away," he explains in his biography. "So my family saw that other guys with the same job I had would do things that I wouldn't. I didn't pay enough attention to my children's individuality. I was not as good a husband as I could have been. A lot of coaches did both of those things very well. I just didn't. That's my biggest regret."[23]

To perform an honest cost-benefit analysis of ambition addiction, however, we need to ask: How many of these coaches, admired by Parcells for shuttling dutifully from home to field to home again, have hoisted the Super Bowl's Lombardi Trophy? Who from that conscientious lot has posed next to a bronze bust of himself in Canton, Ohio, enshrined in the Pro Football Hall of Fame? Could Parcells have attentively parented his own three daughters while also parenting gladiators like linebacker Lawrence Taylor and quarterback Drew Bledsoe? Could he have remained faithful to his wife of forty years while also remaining faithful to the mandates of franchise owners and fans?

We'll never know. What we can say with confidence, however, is that Parcells's ambition enabled him to outpace, outplan, and outplay the competition. He cleared his calendar of extraneous familial concerns, providing extra hours to focus on football, hours that more deferent coaches may have spent at parent-teacher conferences and dates with the old ball and chain. These extra hours delivered him to the Super Bowl. These extra hours enshrined him in the Hall of Fame. Parcells's ambition may have cost him his family, but it won him his wildest dreams.

Another grand master of burning bridges, another ambition addict who achieved his goals at the expense of his loved ones, was billionaire cofounder, chairman, and CEO of Apple Computer, Steve Jobs. To pursue his dreams, to dot the known universe with his signature brand of streamlined delights, Jobs consistently and unabashedly turned his back on anyone who dared slow him down. As Andy Hertzfeld, an Apple engineer and early friend of Jobs, concludes, "Steve is the opposite of loyal. He's anti-loyal. He has to abandon the people he is close to."[24]

Jobs once declared, "You have to have a real single-minded tunnel vision if you want to get anything significant accomplished."[25] This single-minded tunnel vision left little room for the friends, coworkers, and associates he deemed expendable. "Steve never really cared if people thought he was selfish or that his elbows were a little too sharp," writes Brent Schlender, a reporter and friend of Jobs and who interviewed Jobs on numerous occasions. "He was willing to do whatever he felt it took to achieve his goals."[26]

Jobs's "single-minded tunnel vision" enabled him to unreservedly berate subordinates and lambast coexecutives. His harassment turned so fierce, at times, that one manager, Avie Tevanian, took to informing Jobs of any bad news only when Tevanian's team was out of the office.[27] "He didn't dominate you to be mean," explains one of Jobs's mentors, Regis McKenna. "But when people acted as minions, he let them be minions."[28] Walter Isaacson, Jobs's official biographer, adds, "The nasty edge to his personality was not necessary. It hindered him more than it helped him. But it did, at times, serve a purpose. Polite and velvety leaders, who take care to avoid bruising others, are generally not as effective at forcing change."[29]

Some stuck with Jobs, acclimating to his anger, even screaming back themselves. Still, no amount of shared history made one impervious to Jobs's calculating and opportunistic management style. "Steve took shortcuts with people who were close to him," writes Schlender. In the early days, for example, Jobs shortchanged his friend and Apple cofounder Steve Wozniak for earnings the two should have split fifty-fifty.[30] On another occasion, when Apple earnings had climbed into the millions, Jobs refused to give another close friend and early employee, Daniel Kottke, his rightfully earned stock options. Fellow team members objected. One engineer, Rod Holt, pleaded on Kottke's behalf, even offering to match any stock options Jobs was willing to give. In response to Holt, Jobs replied, "Okay, I will give him zero."[31]

Jobs's self-described tunnel vision also left him little bandwidth for the inconveniences of family life. The most profound and heartbreaking example of this came early on when, in his twenties, Jobs discovered that his on-again, off-again girlfriend, Chrisann Brennan, was pregnant. Currently nurturing Apple Computer through its own infancy, Jobs had no time for another dependent. So he said no. No to Brennan. No to fatherhood. No to his child. Elizabeth Holmes, a college friend of Jobs, recalls: "He considered the option of parenthood and considered the option of not being a parent, and he decided to believe the latter. He had other plans for his life."[32] Jobs later summed it up with typical, Zen-like brevity, "I didn't want to be a father, so I wasn't."[33]

Friends and colleagues pushed back. Together with Brennan, they pressed Jobs to take emotional and financial responsibility for his child. Rather than give in to their demands, rather than divide his vision, Jobs fought back. He denied paternity. He accused Brennan of sleeping around. His attorneys obtained blueprints of the house he had once shared with Brennan, hoping to prove how a string of Brennan's supposed lovers might have crawled in and out through a window for midnight rendezvous.[34] Jobs even signed court documents, fraudulently asserting his physical inability to have children.[35]

When all else failed, Jobs settled on a strategy of disengagement. He simply pretended his child did not exist. Isaacson writes, "If reality did not comport with his will, he would ignore it . . ."[36] Adds Schlender, "He was twenty-three years old when Lisa's birth presented him with a clarion call to accept adult responsibility. He rejected the call as fully as he rejected her."[37] After the birth, Jobs didn't even call.[38]

Eventually, Robert Friedland, a close friend of both Jobs and Brennan, confronted Jobs and demanded he visit his child.[39] Jobs acquiesced. He traveled to Friedland's orchard to rendezvous with Brennan and his newborn daughter, Lisa.[40] Yet, this face-to-face meeting with his own flesh and blood did little to change his behavior. Jobs continued to deny paternity and refused to send Brennan assistance. Around the same time that Jobs's earnings reached the million-dollar mark, Brennan and Lisa went on welfare. Later, after a DNA test proved Jobs's paternity, the state of California ordered him to reimburse the state for this welfare subsistence. The state also ordered him to pay Brennan $385 a month in child support, which Jobs, now a multimillionaire, magnanimously rounded up to $500.[41]

A fascinating turn of events, one that helps us understand the machinations of Jobs's ambition-addled mind, occurred in 1985 when he lost his job at Apple. This cataclysmic bump in the road rattled Jobs. For a brief period, he widened his focus, allowing mother and child to enter the frame. His support payments increased. He moved Brennan and Lisa into a nicer home. "I had kept the door open," Brennan recalls, "and when Steve got kicked out of Apple he did find his way into falling in love with Lisa and returning to a friendship with me. . . . Things were different after the power cord between Steve and Apple had been cut."[42]

Soon enough, though, Jobs recovered his professional footing, first at NeXT, then at Lucasfilm, and eventually back in Cupertino. He also married Laurene Powell and became a father thrice more. Yet, despite his billions in the bank and his crowning as the greatest technological visionary of the new millennium, despite a growing family that begged his time and attention, despite his desire not to repeat the paternal sins of the past, Jobs never relaxed his tunnel vision. "He was never destined to win a Father of the Year trophy, even when he had spare time on his hands," Isaacson acknowledges. "He was getting better at paying heed to his children, especially [his son] Reed, but his primary focus was on his work. He was frequently aloof from his two younger daughters, estranged again from Lisa, and often prickly as a husband."[43]

To his dying day, Jobs remained transfixed by his dreams. These dreams placed him not in the valley of the heart, but on the mountaintop of the mind, a stoic sage sculpting pure and perfect technology. Jobs, himself, acknowledged ambition's addictive hold. "I love my family," he once told a reporter while vacationing with them in Hawaii. "And I come here every year. I want to be here. But it's hard for me. I'm always, *always* thinking about Apple."[44]

Ambition addicts possess an uncanny ability to silence the call of the heart. Throughout his life, Jobs slashed and burned, straining or even severing intimate relationships that dared to slow him down. Could he have reached such astronomic heights without this emotional austerity? Would I be typing on my MacBook and texting on my iPhone had he answered the call of the heart? We will never know.

Looking back on that initial decision to abandon his daughter, though, a decision that paved the way for a lifetime of ferocious drive and emotional detachment, of professional dominance and familial sacrifice, Jobs, for his part, expressed regret. "But if I could do it over," he admitted, "I would do a better job."[45]

We ambition addicts may one day find ourselves looking back on our lives and uttering similar sentiments. Having silenced our hearts, having burned our bridges, we may also shoulder the great weight of shame and regret. Unlike Jobs, however, most of us will not have the opportunity to unburden ourselves to our award-winning biographer while lounging on the various verandas of our Palo Alto compound. Having sacrificed relationships for our coveted hopes and dreams, having skipped family dinners and lost touch with loved ones for the sake of our *Any Day Now*, many of us will discover we've bet on a losing proposition. Our emotional sequestration hasn't moved us all that closer to the achievement we seek. All we've gained, in the end, is a life of loneliness and regret, with no one to hear our story and no one to hold our hand.

Our cost-benefit analysis of ambition addiction began with an exploration of how our out-of-control ambition can, and often does, consume the physical body. We can now add a second cost to our ledger. In pursuit of *Any Day Now*, we don't just batter our bodies. We suffocate our hearts. Ambition addiction impairs our capacity to empathize and decreases our devotion to those we love. It strains, and even severs, intimate and cherished relationships. Ambition addiction breaks the bonds of friendship and turns colleagues into combatants. It upends marriages and unravels families. It turns us callous and calculating, fixated on our dreams to the detriment of our own and others' emotional well-being. We may, any day now, burn bright as the stars, but only by placing ourselves against the backdrop of a cold, dark sky.

Building the Pyramids

We've explored how ambition addiction can cripple the body. When we pursue power and glory with ferocious determination, this same rage corrodes our internal anatomy. Ambition addiction pickles our bloodstream in a brine of cortisol and adrenaline. The perpetual stress, the invariable fight-or-flight, thickens our arteries, boils our belly, and frays our nerves. Ambition addiction taxes every major system in our body, propelling us toward the cliff of full-scale physiological collapse.

We've also discussed how ambition addiction can smother the heart. The more savage our drive to succeed, the more willingly we will abandon those who dare disturb our dreams. Colleagues become competitors. Family and friends—dead weight. We deafen our ears and burn our bridges. When our heart objects, we pay it no mind. We focus solely on our own graven image, our ego the only god we dare to obey.

Our cost-benefit analysis of ambition addiction does not end here. Just as ambition addiction taxes us physically and emotionally, it also taxes us spiritually. Whether we realize it or not, whether we believe it or not, we live spiritual lives. Each of us carries a soul within, a spark of divinity, a flicker of eternity bright and brilliant as the sun. The soul comprises our deepest waters; regardless of the storms battering us from without, the soul remains still and untouched within. It is the place, the presence, within us of purity, innocence, truth, faith, and love.

To comprehend how ambition addiction afflicts us spiritually, we must first understand the relationship between the soul and the self. Like a candle's flame, which radiates the physical properties of heat and light, the flame of the soul radiates the spiritual properties of joy and delight. When we walk with a bounce in our step and a smile on our face, when our eyes soften and we know, if only for a moment, that life is good, we have just experienced the reunion of self and soul. The soul has bathed the self in happiness, down to our bones and out through our pores.

All human beings hunger for this soulful happiness. Our longing's deep as DNA. Like our hunger for food, which ensures that nutrients enter our bloodstream, our hunger for happiness ensures that we never stray too far from our deepest selves. Yet, just as nutrients enter our bloodstream only under the right conditions—healthy food synthesized by a properly working digestive tract—this longed-for contact of self and soul can take place only under the right conditions, as well.

To satiate our hunger for happiness, to reunite with our soul, we need to cultivate three qualities: a relaxed body, a loving heart, and an attentive mind. The body, heart, and mind act as lenses, each lens nesting one against the next. When we make choices that relax our body, stimulate our heart, and focus our mind, we remove accumulated smudges and schmutz from each lens. The lenses turn translucent; radiant joy passes right through body, heart, and mind on its journey from soul to self.

When, on the other hand, we experience fear, when our nerves tense, our heart palpitates, and our synapses spasm, the lenses of body, heart, and mind cloud over. Our essential being turns opaque. The flame of our soul burns just as bright as it always has, but a grimy film of fear prevents our ability to see it, to feel it, to know it. This obscured radiance starves us of the happiness we seek. Fear robs us of contact with our deepest wisdom and our most abundant joy.

The activities, settings, and people that relax my body, open my heart, and focus my mind are not the same activities, settings, and people that relax your body, open your heart, and focus your mind. Each of us satiates our hunger for happiness by whipping up a unique stew of the self, an individualized mixture of identity and activity that we hope will stick to our ribs. A hedge fund manager eyeing a portfolio and a loinclothed renunciant contemplating a flower have cooked very different stews; yet, even with a dramatically different palate of ingredients, each cooks with similar intentions. Each yearns for a relaxed body, an open heart, and a focused mind. Each hopes to satisfy the same grumbling in the gut. Through diverse means, each works toward the same end: a soulful happiness, deep and true.

Not all of us conceive of happiness as the radiance of soul. Some of us imagine happiness as an external effervescence, a vapor emanating from the people, places, and things that delight. Happiness does not originate within, this theory suggests. Happiness enters from without, infusing our senses, rushing through our bloodstream, and triggering a symphony of serotonin. Those of us with this belief tend to spend as much time as possible with high-risk equities, dewdropped flowers, or whatever else we've identified as a wellspring of joy. The closer we get to these people, places, and things, the more they will shower mists of happiness upon us.

This notion, that something or someone outside ourselves can "make us happy," is a fallacy. Hedge funding and flower gazing don't make hedge funders and flower gazers happy. Hedge funding and flower gazing dissipate fear. These activities relax the body, head, and heart, creating the right conditions for what actually "makes us happy"—the radiance of the soul. If our hedge fund manager and our loinclothed renunciant understand this, if they perceive the true mechanism of happiness, if they know that joy abides within, available at any moment of relaxation, openheartedness, and attention, they may still opt for a life of investment portfolios and wildflowers. These passions provide dependable routes to relaxation, devotion, and engagement. However, when it's time to leave the office or descend from the mountain, they won't despair. Our hedge funder and renunciant recognize that happiness is sourced from soul, not from circumstance. They can adore their spreadsheets and spring blooms; yet, when other obligations arise, when the family gathers for dinner or the visa renewal's due, they can step back from their passions. They can courageously open their bodies, hearts, and minds to a different milieu. Life may have temporarily robbed them of a few of their favorite things; still, happiness is available to them whenever and wherever they can relax, engage, and enjoy.

If, on the other hand, our hedge funder and renunciant attribute happiness to hedge funding and flower gazing alone, they will resent any occasion when they must turn off the computer, stand up from the meadow, and enter a less idyllic locale. They will resent the people, places, and things that appear to rob them of happiness. Dinner at the hedge fund manager's home may involve a pack of untamed offspring and a singularly irritating spouse. Obtaining a visa at the consulate may require our renunciant to endure hours, if not days, of soul-crushing bureaucracy. Believing that happiness exists "back there" at the office, or "up there" on the mountain, the manager and the monk will hold their breath at the dinner table and in the consulate's long line. They will try to just get through it. Rather than live, they will endure. And, as soon as the table's cleared and the passport's stamped, they will scramble back to their beloved funds and flowers.

When we omit the soul from the schematics of delight, we plant the seed of addiction. Rather than cultivating inner reserves of relaxation, love, and mindfulness, we cling to catalysts. We chase without what we possess within. Over time, this can transform us into dependent, inflexible, and desperate creatures, forever aching for that next fix. What began as an innocent attraction, a passion for hedge funds, a preference for mountain blooms, a love of buying, selling, painting, parenting, meditating, ministering, dating, or dieting, has morphed into an obsession.

The more we feed an addiction, any addiction, the more we lose the ability to delight in our drug of choice. The mechanism of happiness, the alignment of body, heart, and mind, the transmission of the light of the soul, this complex internal apparatus shuts down in the presence of fear. Desperation disables our ability to rejoice and delight. When that hedge fund manager erroneously concludes that hedge funding makes her happy, when she clings to hedge funding to get high, she may start to fret—what if I get fired? What if the economy tanks? Will I ever be happy again? As for our blissed-out beatnik in the Himalayas, he, like his corporate counterpart, has gotten nervous. What if he gets word (schlepped via Sherpa) that a family member has fallen ill? What if his host country revokes his visa? What will he do without the mountains, the flowers, the sunsets, the silence? How will he survive at low altitudes? As anxiety metastasizes, less and less happiness finds its way past tangled nerves, hardened hearts, and panic-stricken minds.

If this situation weren't bleak enough, what happens when we add ambition to the mix? What happens when we crave not only high-yield investments, high-altitude tranquility, or whatever else we erroneously believe "makes us happy," but we also set our sights on all-encompassing glory? What happens when we look to the stars as the true source of joy?

When we turned to the soul for satisfaction, we were free to wander and wonder. We could follow our passions, but we could also take a walk in the park, sip tea, paddle a canoe, or swoosh down a slope. Happiness could be realized anytime, anywhere, as long as we relaxed. When we then began to look outside ourselves for happiness, we relinquished some of this freedom. We limited our flight paths to preapproved destinations; we allowed our passions to confine us, convinced that happiness must be gathered from without, not realized within. Now, as we begin to look for happiness in the achievement of all-or-nothing, objectified goals, when we cling to our *Any Day Now* as our joy and salvation, we lose our last degree of autonomy, flexibility, and freedom. No more sipping tea. No more paddling canoes. No more adventures and surprises. Our raging, ruthless ambition cracks the whip. Our very dreams enslave us. Chained to fantasy, bereft of joy, we ambition addicts bow and obey.

To study the life of tastemaker and media mogul Martha Stewart is to witness this spiritual enslavement, this erosion of autonomy, flexibility, and freedom. On the surface, we behold an American dream fulfilled: a daughter of middle-class, Polish immigrants who, through a combination of intelligence, determination, and creativity, turned her tiny catering business into a multibillion-dollar corporation. We eye an ambitious alpha, envied and feared, surrounded by legions of admirers and riches galore. In Stewart, we see the fame and fortune that comes from addictive, single-minded ambition. We squint from the glare of glorious dreams fulfilled. Stewart stands before us tireless and triumphant, a connoisseur of culture, a goddess of house and home.

However, as with all things Stewart, one would be wise to look behind the curtain. The Martha of charming decor is also the Martha marched off to prison. The Martha posh and polished is also the Martha bereft and abandoned. It's fitting, really, that long before her rise to royalty, Stewart named her first catering business "The Uncatered Affair."[46] The more Thanksgiving turkeys and manicured lawns she broadcast around the globe, the more her own world transformed from dream to disillusionment. A slave to her ambition, Stewart's life descended into an uncatered affair.

"Martha always won," writes longtime friend and neighbor Mariana Pasternak in her 2010 book *The Best of Friends: Martha and Me*.[47] In the years Pasternak and Stewart spent side by side, taking family vacations together, promoting each other's work, and investing in each other's success, Pasternak watched how Stewart's "insatiable desire for power" transformed her once "audacious and uninhibited" friend, her friend "always ready for an adventure," into a humorless and heavy-hearted workaholic.[48]

According to Pasternak, Stewart's ambition, her insatiable desire for power, appeared to own her, every minute of every day. "[Martha] worked nonstop," Pasternak recalls, "often short-tempered, her body took on a rigid new mien, the spring in her step faded, her waist thickened, and her hands seemed permanently clenched as though always grasping for something."[49] Like a slave, who has no control over their time, who can never say, "Phew, I've worked for twelve hours straight—time for a break," Stewart lost all control of time. Jumping at the crack of ambition's whip, she didn't dare rest.

Others began to notice Stewart's inability to pause, rest, and make time for anything other than her expanding empire. Writes biographer Christopher Byron:

> As Martha's fame grew, and she became increasingly absorbed in making it grow still more, she seemed to have less and less time available for her personal relationships—not just with [her husband] Andy and [her daughter] Alexis, but with her employees, her neighbors, and anyone else she might encounter day to day. A brusque efficiency began to take over her conversations. People remarked on how Martha would end conversations by simply walking away, or by hanging up the telephone without even saying goodbye.[50]

Enslaved by her dreams, her life no longer her own, Stewart could spare no time for simple greetings and salutations. Ambition steered her every move.

"[Stewart] had become one of the busiest, most hyperactive women in America," writes Byron. To many, Stewart's life appeared bleak and joyless. Though she squeezed out contented smiles for the camera, her apparent misery, so ubiquitous, so palpable, became the talk of the town. "Rarely has America produced a public figure who appears more tortured than Martha Stewart," adds Byron. "Martha's personal behavior became the elephant in the room that nobody wanted to discuss."[51]

Ambition starved Stewart of joy, blinded her with desperation, and enslaved her to dreams of power and glory. This obsession culminated in her decision, in 2001, to utilize an illegal stock tip to avoid losing $45,000 in the market. Just a year earlier, Stewart had been crowned the first female, self-made billionaire in US history. She had perched upon an unparalleled empire of fame, fortune, power, and prestige. Yet, to protect a negligible percentage of her net worth, Stewart risked it all. Thus, the great, untouchable epicure found herself the recipient of a year in court, three felony convictions, a $200,000 fine, and five months behind bars.

Over the years, many of us have watched Martha Stewart transform mundane materials into impeccable delicacies, all the while conceding that our own disorderly lives could never so easily transform. Stewart has even engendered resentment from some; she epitomizes the too-good-to-be-true bubble we're dying to burst. When we view Stewart's story through the lens of ambition addiction, however, we see a woman in chains. Smothered beneath opportunism and hyperactivity, a heart still beats. A soul still shines. Joy, contentment, and gratitude call out for release. By viewing Stewart not as maniacal or malicious, but as one who gradually relinquished her freedom for the sake of her dreams, we humanize her. We place ourselves, as fellow, fallible human beings, by her side. Martha's mistakes could be our own. When we prize dreams of domination over the soulful happiness of a relaxed, openhearted, mindful life, we, like Stewart, risk losing our freedom. We, like Stewart, risk enslavement to our dreams. Our time no longer our own, our lives no longer our own, we, like Stewart, risk forgetting how to say "hello" and "good-bye."

Indeed, as we conclude our cost-benefit analysis, as we contemplate the astronomical ascendency and disastrous deterioration of individuals like Parcells, Jobs, and Stewart, we would be wise not to view any of them at a distance. To diagnose ourselves as ambition addicts is to declare, "I am Bill Parcells. I am Steve Jobs. I am Martha Stewart." We have their drive and focus. We possess their rage. While there are no guarantees, while many of us may reach for the stars only to fall short, over and over again, a few of us, like Parcells, Jobs, and Stewart, may even, any day now, get what we want.

On the other hand, if we are Parcells, Jobs, and Stewart, reaping the benefits of our rage, we are also Parcells, Jobs, and Stewart, forced to pay the piper. We may reach the Hall of Fame, but we may get there with arteries tightening, stomachs spewing, and bodies minute by minute closing in on collapse. We may invent and innovate, bold and brilliant, but we may accomplish this by berating our colleagues, abusing our friends, and abandoning our spouses, daughters, and sons. We may ascend to royalty, rich and renowned; yet, we will wear our crowns in misery and terror, bowing before our *Any Day Now* as dutiful slaves.

Alcoholics intone the requisite "I am an alcoholic," regardless of how many decades they've gone without a drink. Ambition addiction works the same way. Every day, we ambition addicts must open our eyes and acknowledge our lot. We start by telling the truth: "I am an ambition addict." The truth then sets us free, and with that freedom we make a choice. Will we indulge our addiction today, pursuing our fantasies and reaching for glory no matter the costs? Or, today, will we choose a different path? A path of honesty. A path of courage. A path of recovery.

We are ambition addicts. We are Parcells. We are Jobs. We are Stewart. And here we are, my brothers and sisters, ready to choose. Will we put this book down so we can reach for the stars? Or will we take a deep breath, gather our courage, and turn the page?

PART II

The Road to Recovery

Step One

Slow Down

We ambition addicts dream very different dreams. We navigate diverse and disparate worlds. Yet, all of us, no matter the activity, venue, or great and glorious goal, have at least one behavior in common—we are running for our lives.

Why do we run? Why are we in such a hurry all the time? Why do we lunge at breakneck speed toward each triumphant victory? Does it really matter if we arrive at our *Any Day Now* today, tomorrow, or a year from now? What's the rush?

Since we're likely in a hurry at this very moment, let's start with a quick and easy answer. We rush through our lives because *Any Day Now*, looking so excruciatingly, orgasmically, eyes-rolled-back-in-the-head delicious, dangles just out of reach. We can't wait to dive headfirst into its garden of earthly delights. We run hungry, with too many hoops pockmarking our path. Every time we jump through one hoop, praying it will be the last, another one appears. And then another. And another. Ages ago, we undertook this enterprise with a rumbling in our belly.

Now, we're starving. If we don't cross that finish line soon, we feel like we're going to die. What choice do we have? Better pick up the pace.

This answer—that we rush through our lives to catch up with our dreams—is true but incomplete. There is another explanation for our frantic pace, some additional catalysts that, at this very moment, bear down on us from behind. I refer to, of course, our oh-so-favorite three-some—*Uncertainty, Vulnerability, and Mortality*. We may run to reach the stars. We may race to wear the crown. Even without *Any Day Now*'s carrot dangling before our eyes, however, we would still careen around every curve. Our demons keep us dancing on coals, never stabile, never still, leaping and lurching and forever on the run.

We ambition addicts rush through our lives propelled not by one force, but by two. *Any Day Now* tugs us from the front. *Uncertainty, Vulnerability, and Mortality* push us from behind. We are tiny ships engulfed by gale-force winds—what choice do we have? We run. We sprint through e-mails and meetings. We speed through bedtime with the kids. We bump carts with an old friend in the produce aisle, and, when they ask how we're doing, we open our eyes wide, feign a great sigh, and answer, "BUSY!" Then we do everything possible to wrap up the reunion before it begins. We just don't have time! Our dreams await. Our demons descend.

The relationship between our dreams and our demons involves more than mere collaboration, however. Our demons give birth to our dreams. As we embark upon the road to recovery, then, as we prepare to decelerate, we begin at the beginning, at the point where, once upon a time, our demons drew close and we broke into a run. This initial step on the road to recovery does not directly address the details of our *Any Day Now*. We'll deconstruct our dreams eventually; first, though, we need to *Slow Down*, to learn how to tolerate our pursuers' proximity. By turning to face the chaos of *Uncertainty*, the shame of *Vulnerability*, and the terror of *Mortality*, by circumventing our ego and confronting our fears, we start cultivating wellsprings of strength, wisdom, and compassion. These are exactly the qualities we will need when, later on down the road, we turn back to assess our happy endings.

To *Slow Down*, to keep from bolting as the trio of *Uncertainty, Vulnerability, and Mortality* approach, we enlist the help of a very different trio—the trio of *Breath, Word, and Deed*.

To understand how *Breath, Word, and Deed* work, let's pay a visit to our old buddy Al. Remember Al, Al the ambition addict, the one who longed for billions in the bank and a tabloid-worthy physique? Al had thought *Any Day Now* would deliver him the world of his dreams. Of late, though, his relentless work and over-the-top workouts have caused him, and those around him, a whole lot of grief. His wife's grown bitter, rarely meeting his eyes. His colleagues, sensing his cutthroat intentions, have turned on him at work. After every red-faced, rage-filled workout, his knees, elbows, shoulders, and back have started to seize up. Sometimes, he can hardly move.

Al needs to make a change. He wants to break the cycle of ambition addiction before his wife leaves him, his coworkers take him down, and his body falls to pieces. Al's ready to embark upon the road to recovery.

Step one—he needs to *Slow Down*.

To *Slow Down*, Al utilizes the technique of *Breath, Word, and Deed*. He can practice this technique anywhere, anytime. As it so happens, he's decided to try it out at the gym, right in the middle of his bench-press routine. To practice *Breath, Word, and Deed*, Al begins by simply noticing his breath. As he lowers and raises the bench-press bar, he observes each inhalation as it inflates his chest. He feels each exhalation explode from his puffed-up cheeks. Al doesn't manipulate his breath. He doesn't try to breathe faster or slower. He doesn't worry about pairing the breath with certain movements. He simply watches the breath. Like a driver on a coastal highway who's pulled off to enjoy the ocean view, Al's momentarily detoured from his usual fixations, paying homage to the ever-present, yet rarely accentuated, tide of his breath.

Having wedded consciousness with breath, Al moves on to the next stage of *Breath, Word, and Deed.* Paired with each inhalation and exhalation, Al begins to recite a succinct play-by-play of each action he performs. On his next inhalation, for instance, he thinks to himself, "I am lowering the bench-press bar." On his exhalation, he thinks to himself, "I am raising the bench-press bar." Again, inhaling, he thinks, "I am lowering the bench-press bar." Exhaling, he thinks, "I am raising the bench-press bar." If, after a few repetitions, he changes his activity, if he puts down the bar and grabs a drink of water, Al simply adjusts his narration. Inhaling, he thinks, "I am putting down the bench-press bar." Exhaling, he thinks, "I am sitting up." Inhaling, "I am grabbing my water bottle." Exhaling, "I am drinking water."

This simple act of weaving breath, narration, and action transforms Al, both physiologically and psychologically. Physiologically, *Breath, Word, and Deed* reverses Al's fight-or-flight feedback loop. Before, when Al amped himself up on ambition, he triggered a regularly scheduled release of cortisol and adrenaline. These stress hormones gave him a better buzz than a hipster-brewed latte. They encouraged him to accelerate his speed, increase his output, boost his confidence, enlarge his dreams, and then send these juiced-up dreams once more through his nervous system, triggering an even greater surge of fight-or-flight.

With the introduction of *Breath, Word, and Deed*, however, Al reverses the cycle. As long as he focuses on the present moment, providing a play-by-play of his actions, he refrains from sending messages like "I will become Matthew McConaughey" to his already flustered limbic system. His limbic system, sensing a change in the air, responds by taking things down from DEFCON 5. No more *Threat!* messages. No new surge of hormones. If Al can stay with the technique another, say, twenty or thirty minutes, he will give his body enough time to reabsorb any lingering stress hormones floating through his bloodstream. This absorption of old hormones combined with the absence of new hormones will, eventually, shift Al from hyperdrive to easy does it, not only in his outlook, but beneath his skin as well.

Psychologically, *Breath, Word, and Deed* yanks Al's mind back from future fantasy to present reality. Al's so busy juggling breaths, words, and deeds, he can't spare the bandwidth for thoughts of swooning admirers or a chiseled McConaughey. As the practice peels away this thin veneer of *Any Day Now* from before his eyes, it reveals the richness of the present moment. The bench-press bar hovers above Al's chest and, for the first time, he sees the crisscross indentations along the bar's grips. He hears that crappy pop song blaring through the gym's speakers. He feels a subtle ache that's developed in his right shoulder. The obstacle of ambition momentarily removed, Al's mind and body unite, allowing the sensations of the moment to flood his consciousness. As consciousness merges with moment, Al feels less anxious and agitated. He bench-presses with focus and determination, but also with a sense of peace and well-being. He's relaxed even in the midst of exertion. He breaks a sweat but his eyes stay soft; his jaw stays loose.

This physiological and psychological transformation, this shift from fight-or-flight desperation to calm-and-collected attention, decelerates Al. He can't seem to barrel through his bench presses the way he could when, with each breath, he thought, "I will become Matthew McConaughey . . . I will make women swoon . . . I will become Matthew McConaughey . . . I will make women swoon." His body's relaxed. His mind has released thoughts of the future and merged with the moment. All this has transformed his workout from an exercise he must hurriedly endure, from a painful means to a glorious end, into an experience to engage, a moment to behold, nice and slow, breath by breath.

As we begin to explore this practice of *Breath, Word, and Deed*, as we start to *Slow Down*, we may find ourselves asking, "How long do I have to do this?" The practice can feel tedious, frustrating, or downright boring. We don't really want to pour ourselves a bowl of cereal each morning and think, "I am pouring a bowl of cereal." Wedding the mundane actions of our routine lives to a golf-announcer-style narration in our head may, at times, feel like a punishment—a little like watching paint dry, right?

So, pun very much intended, we take it slow. We don't practice all the time. With sanity as our objective, why drive ourselves nuts? We can start the practice with a reasonable, realistic goal, something like: *Every time I feel like I need to go faster and faster, to get it all done before the world undoes me, I'll practice* Breath, Word, and Deed *for five minutes.* The practice is a tool. When we need the tool, we use it. When we don't need it, we put it down. I find that, as an ambition addict, I need the practice every day, but not every minute of every day. Sometimes, my mind and body agreeably unwind within the present moment, no need for any external encouragement. Other times, a lot of the time, it's back to the drawing board: "I am stirring a pot of noodles . . . I am reading to my daughter . . . I am typing on the keys . . . I am walking to my car . . ."

Whenever we practice *Breath, Word, and Deed*, whenever we pull our consciousness out of the fantastical future and into present reality, we need to prepare ourselves for what's headed our way. As we slow ourselves down, narrating our every move, hovering in the present moment, *Uncertainty, Vulnerability, and Mortality* have been gaining on us. Remember, we devoted our lives to *Any Day Now* in order to escape these antagonists. We've spent decades on the run, all in an effort to outpace their approach. Now, on the road to recovery, we've started to slow. But they haven't. And it may take only a minute or two of thinking, "I am stirring a pot of noodles . . ." before we feel our demons' hot, fetid breath on the back of our necks.

With this in mind, let's check in with Al to see how he's doing. Back at the gym, Al's managed to keep *Breath, Word, and Deed* going while finishing his bench presses, and even while walking to the locker room, showering, toweling off, and getting dressed. Not bad for a rookie. In fact, as we peek in on him now, he's putting on his shoes, just about ready to leave. Sitting on the locker-room bench, putting one shoe on his foot, he thinks, "I am putting on my shoe." Crossing one rabbit ear over the other, he thinks, "I am tying my shoe." Reaching for his other shoe, he prepares to intone the play-by-play. And that's when, out of nowhere, *Uncertainty* strikes.

"Al!" *Uncertainty* whispers. "Hey! Al!"

"I am putting on my shoe," Al answers.

"Al," *Uncertainty* continues, undeterred, "you remember Bruce Goldings? Yeah, you know, Bruce, your supervisor, that schmuck who used to wear bow ties on Fridays? Whatever happened to old Bruce? Oh yeah, now I remember. He got fired, didn't he?"

Al loses his train of thought. *Bruce Goldings? Man, I haven't thought about him for a while.*

Uncertainty continues, "I mean, you never know what's coming your way, do you? Here's Bruce, showing up to the office one morning, and before he knows it, he's gotten the old heave-ho. Packed his desk, packed his bags, packed his life. I think he ended up finding a gig in Des Moines. Wow . . . Des Moines. Crazy how things like that can happen, isn't it, Al? One day, you're inches from the corner office. Then you feel like you need a change. You read some new-age bullshit about living a more balanced life and so you decide to slow things down a bit. Seems harmless, right? Then BAM! You're bouncing through Des Moines trailing a U-Haul!"

Or, maybe *Uncertainty* doesn't get to Al first. Maybe it's *Vulnerability* who elbows her way to the front of the line.

"Al," *Vulnerability* coos, "Al, sweetie. I'm not interrupting anything, am I?"

"I am putting on my shoe," Al repeats, squinting his eyes, trying to bring his shoe into focus.

"Al, I don't mean to be a bother, but I happened to notice that today you took it easy with those bench presses. Now, darling, we've talked about this before. It's unfortunate, what happened to you in sixth grade, but it's a reality we have to confront. You had breasts, dear. Actual tits. The envy of every prepubescent girl! You were so heavy that those bullies used to tackle you, lift up your shirt, and slap your belly until your skin turned pink. Do you remember that, Al? Do you hear their laughter? Can you feel the sting? We can't afford to go slow, Al, not with a fatty inside us, a fatty who could leap out any second, breasts and all!"

Or perhaps *Mortality*'s the one to catch Al off guard.

"I am putting on my shoe," Al intones, starting to slip the second shoe over his toes. Then, he feels something, a passing shadow, a subtle shift of the light. Al looks up from his shoe. He stares at his locker. He hears the ambient noise of conversations, blow-dryers, and flushing toilets, but everything's suddenly muffled, distant, as if his head is wrapped in gauze.

Al starts to feel small. Small and insignificant. Small and insignificant and old.

What am I doing? What the hell am I doing? I'm forty-seven years old. I'm still a nobody, a random guy in a random town, pushing papers around my desk as the seconds tick away. What's the point? Why does it matter? Why do I matter? I've done nothing with my life. Nothing. When I die, no one will even remember my name.

Whether from *Uncertainty*'s intrusions, *Vulnerability*'s assault, or *Mortality*'s silent stare, Al forgets all about *Breath, Word, and Deed.* His stomach starts to ache. A wave of edginess rolls up his spine. His shoulders tighten. His heart rate soars. He finishes tying his shoes, but with a tight-jawed determination. *There's no way I'm getting fired and ending up in Des Moines! I won't let myself get fat again, forget that! I'd rather rush through every minute of every day before I let myself die a no-name schlub with a one-line obituary.* Al's panicked. He's gotta get out of here, out of this present moment, before it's too late!

And that's when (cue chorus of celestial voices) he sees it. A marquee bathed in warm, bright light. A sanctuary promising shelter from the storm. *Any Day Now*'s open for business. Al ties his shoe, grabs his gym bag, and breaks into a run.

By practicing *Breath, Word, and Deed*, by uniting our mind with our body in the present moment and *Slowing Down*, what we've kept buried starts bubbling to the surface. When we *Slow Down*, our demons catch up. They've been waiting for just this opportunity. Old traumas, anxiety, and angst fill our field of vision. We feel edgy, impatient, angry, morose, exhausted, panicked, needy, lonely, or resentful. Even just a minute of *Breath, Word, and Deed* can make us want to crawl out of our skin, like we're sitting in the fire, like we're dying. And nothing, at this moment, would feel better than running away as fast as we possibly can.

So, as we begin our practice of *Breath, Word, and Deed*, we need to remember: We are addicts and this is detox. We've lost our capacity to face *Uncertainty*, experience *Vulnerability*, and contemplate *Mortality*. Our hair-trigger system shuts down at the merest hint of existential truth. When we start to detox, then, purging stale perspectives and modifying problematic behaviors, we expose our sheltered selves to the elements. We introduce new movement to old, immovable joints. We hurt as we heal.

The road to recovery is not meant to kill us, however, but to set us free. So when demons descend, and descend they will, when *Slowing Down* starts to feel like hell on earth, I recommend we do the following. First, no matter the pain, we continue the practice of *Breath, Word, and Deed* for three more cycles of inhalations and exhalations—no more, no less. These may feel like the longest three breaths we've ever taken, but we don't dare give up. Then, after these three breaths, we stop. We let the practice go for a while. We even break into a run.

Eventually, after a few minutes, or a few hours, or whenever we notice ourselves once more out of breath and out of time, we return to the practice. Inhaling, "I am driving to the grocery store." Exhaling, "I am driving to the grocery store." Inhaling, "I am parking the car." Exhaling, "I am parking the car." When the edgy uneasiness returns, when the only play-by-play we can offer is: inhaling, "I hate this fucking practice," exhaling, "I think I'll drive right off that cliff," we don't give up. Not quite yet. This time round, we keep it going for four more breaths. Four laborious, excruciating, torturous breaths. Then, once again, we stop.

From four breaths, we go to five. From five breaths, to six. And onward we go. Eventually, we'll hold to the present moment for twenty breaths, or even thirty. *Uncertainty, Vulnerability, and Mortality* will perch on our shoulders, reach down our throats, and tie our guts into knots, but, for those twenty or thirty breaths, we won't run away. We will face our demons. We will stand our ground.

Detox doesn't last forever. We'll always have moments, of course, born from inner life or outer circumstance, that send us fleeing from our demons and running for the marquee. Yet, even at these moments, when we recover our composure and return to our practice, we won't necessarily feel like we've been raked over the coals. It may take months, or even years, but, eventually, we will purge our bloodstreams of surplus hormones and acclimate ourselves to a decelerated status quo. After a while, we may even find ourselves slipping into *Breath, Word, and Deed* without realizing it, slow and steady our new normal.

The more we practice, the more our demons will retreat. But they never disappear. For the rest of our lives, they will resort to flinging lackluster incitements in our direction, little barbs we will learn to endure first for three breaths, then for four, and then for five. The attacks will sting, but only for a moment. We may even chuckle to ourselves, thinking, "There they go again, my silly little demons, up to no good." Then, shaking our heads, we will continue with our day.

In the midst of our *Slowing Down*, as we do our best to withstand our demons within, we may also encounter pushback from without. While some of our friends, family, colleagues, and community members had grown frustrated attempting to flag us down, others had profited from our pace. Before beginning our recovery, we may have gravitated to individuals, perhaps ambition addicts themselves, who maintain an equally hurried velocity. Some of these individuals may not only expect our fever pitch, they may rely on it. Our boss expects to see us screaming down the hallways at a fast clip. Our friends enjoy life served up at seventy miles an hour, running from club to club or café to café, drinking fast, talking fast, bouncing from topic to topic like a news ticker on CNN. Even our spouse finds our attempted deceleration disconcerting. Why can't we, in the thirty minutes before dinner, fit in five more errands and answer ten more texts? What's taking us so long?

We may decide, with some individuals, that we want to come clean. "I've got a problem," we can say to friends and family. "I'm an ambition addict. I've been driving myself and a lot of other people crazy. I've been running myself ragged and making myself, and maybe you, too, miserable. I want to make a change. I want to be healthy and happy. So I've decided to take a breath and *Slow Down*." To a boss or colleague, to acquaintances and neighbors, we don't necessarily have to advertise our addiction or familiarize others with the road to recovery. We could respond to queries with "You know, I've been moving way too fast these days. I feel like I'm a chicken running around with its head cut off. I want to experience my life. I want to take my time with the things that matter—family, friends, work. So I'm trying something new these days. I'm breathing. I'm living in the moment. I'm going slow."

Those who love us, those who value us not only for what we produce, but for who we are, will hear these words and honor this development. They will note our more relaxed demeanor, the absence of panic in our eyes. Hearing us laugh for the first time in ages, they may even think to themselves, "Wow. She seems great. He's so relaxed. Maybe I should slow down, too." As for those who feel threatened by our attempted recovery, as for the individuals who much preferred us dizzy and dialed up, all we can do is reassure them, as best we can, that we'll still do our job. We'll still try our best. Who knows? As we learn to act more thoughtfully and focus more mindfully, our *Slowing Down* may even, in the long run, improve our productivity. And, by lowering our blood pressure, it may boost our longevity, too.

Slowing Down is hard work. For ambition addicts, however, *Slowing Down* is the fundamental first step toward recovery. By modulating our tempo from hyperdrive to easy does it, by shifting our attention from fantasized future to present reality, we allow our bodies to rest. We invite our minds to engage. We make space for our souls to shine. The soul couldn't catch us when we used to go whizzing by. Now, when we tie our shoes, we do it slowly. We feel our breath flow in and out. We watch the laces cross and loop. We caress the material between our fingers and hear the narration dance through our head. We greet the moment and the moment responds, filling our senses, rushing in. It calls to the soul and out pours the light, a light far brighter than *Any Day Now*'s marquee. In this light, we see ourselves and our world for the miracles they are. In this light, we don't fear, we rejoice.

Step Two

Enjoy

A few years ago, Carnival Cruise Line ran a television ad that opens with a girl, probably twelve or thirteen, walking around a corner and stopping dead in her tracks. She stares at something in the distance, her eyes wide with disbelief. A pink bubble of chewing gum balloons from her lips, mirroring her widening eyes, turning her mouth into an exaggerated *O* of shock. The camera then cuts to the source of her astonishment. A clean-shaven, slightly balding man, probably in his forties, wearing a blue dress shirt unbuttoned to his chest, stands in the middle of a nightclub dance floor, leaping and hollering with unfettered jubilation. An equally exuberant woman, wearing a sleeveless dress and sporting a sensibly cropped head of red hair, bounces next to her man.

"What's going on with Dad?" a deep, disembodied voice asks, presumably narrating the thoughts running through gum-chewing girl's head. Cut to another shot of the dancing man, now running through the unpaved streets of some unnamed tropic locale. Cut again to Dad frolicking at the pool, then trying on goofy sunglasses with the girl, then snapping his wife's tush with a towel as she, giggling enticingly, goes to close their cabin's bedroom door. All the while the narration continues, "Dad seems different. He's not talking about work. He's not tucking in his shirt. He's not checking messages every nine seconds. And now this?" Back to a shot of Dad on the dance floor, strumming an air guitar and kicking a flip-flopped foot high into the air. The ad concludes with a final close-up of the daughter, still in shock, the pink bubble of gum finally bursting upon her lips.

What's going on with Dad? We, the viewers of said commercial, have no trouble answering this question. Dad's unplugged. Dad's decompressed. Dad's boarded a self-enclosed, seafaring sanctuary, all hands on deck dedicated to his prepaid, all-inclusive, all-encompassing enjoyment. Dad's gone from furious commute along congested beltways to gentle cruise through Caribbean tides. The tempered pace aboard the ship hems him in, yet he feels freer. The Internet connection's spotty, yet he feels more connected than he ever did back on terra firma. A blue expanse of time and space, sea and sky, spreads before him, and with every inhalation and exhalation, maritime air cleanses him, refreshes him, stimulates his senses, and revives his soul. What's going on with Dad? Dad's cruising, and with a little help from an army of attendants, rediscovering how to *Enjoy*.

Like the dad in the commercial, we ambition addicts have pursued our dreams by keeping ourselves tightly wound and buttoned up. Our "work," whether it takes place at the office, at our home, or in the carpool line at our children's school, consumes us. We check our smartphones every few seconds. We can't unwind without a drink. Our daughters and sons may well have forgotten what we look like dancing to disco, or goofing around in the pool, or trying on silly hats just for fun. Our spouses may have assumed we'd buried our raucous, randy, grab-a-quickie-in-the-shower mojo beneath mountains of paperwork and e-mails.

But then, on the road to recovery, we slow down. We downshift, not by booking a ticket on an actual cruise, but by imposing upon ourselves an equally confining yet blissfully liberating internal environment: *Breath, Word, and Deed.* The practice of *Breath, Word, and Deed* takes us out to sea. It slows our fever pitch with its own version of cocktails and calypso. We find ourselves perched on the bow of our own private vessel, body relaxed, mind present, the great expanse of time and space extending out to the horizon.

It is at this point, cruising slow and steady, learning to share tight quarters with fellow cruisers *Insecurity, Vulnerability, and Mortality*, that we can turn to step two on the road to recovery. We are prepared not only to *Slow Down*, but to take a gander at the recreational offerings available on the lido deck. We are available to do a little dance, make a little love, smell the flowers, and bask in the sun. We are ready to *Enjoy*.

We ambition addicts operate under the assumption that the future should, and will, be more enjoyable than the present. Any day now, we will free ourselves from this DMV waiting room of a life and, number called, ticket punched, exit into sunshine and open air. If we put our nose to the grindstone and get a firm grip on our bootstraps, this frequently confusing, invariably disheartening, occasionally distressing existence will assuredly transform. The waiting room gray will disappear. *Insecurity, Vulnerability, and Mortality* will take a hike. All our glorious dreams will manifest, and life will resemble a Caribbean cruise.

Enjoy, the second step on our road to recovery, subverts this paradigm. Rather than tantalize us with promises of a better tomorrow, *Enjoy* invites us to relax and delight, not tomorrow, not this afternoon, but now. Right now. And if, right now, we happen to be wincing in the dentist's chair in the midst of a tooth extraction, *Enjoy* reminds us that, when the Novocain wears off, we're due for a massage. Or a nice walk in the park. Or an ice cream cone, cavities be damned. Not any day now. Now.

We ambition addicts may argue that reaching for the stars brings us enjoyment galore. We've chosen the specifics of our striving for good reason. We buy, sell, paint, parent, meditate, minister, date, or diet because we love these activities. We get a contact high just from gazing at our day planners and viewing today's docket of potential pursuits. We don't suffer from a lack of enjoyment. We suffer from an inability to regulate our appetite. How will a prescription for sensual indulgence, how will an ice cream cone or a walk in the park, curb compulsion? If anything, a prescription for ice cream cones and walks in the park may compound our symptoms, turning us into ambition addicts who spend even less time with our loved ones; now, when not competing for gold, we're gorging on desserts or tiptoeing through the tulips.

The hedonistic highs of ice cream cones and afternoon strolls, however, operate quite differently from ambition-driven enjoyment. When we dive into cookies and cream, we indulge not to fulfill our hopes and dreams, but because, right here, right now, it tastes so damn good. The thrill of ambition, on the other hand, involves a complex amalgam of immediate gratification and future-oriented aspiration. When we buy, sell, paint, parent, meditate, minister, date, or diet, we derive enjoyment from the activity itself, but we also derive enjoyment from the *idea* of the activity. We delight in the significance of our struggle and striving.

For individuals with healthy levels of ambition, this blend of pleasure and purpose, sensual delight and conceptual relevance, can infuse life with meaning and contentment. Harvard psychologist Tal Ben-Shahar goes so far as to identify ambitious activity, when circumscribed appropriately and actualized mindfully, as the very definition of happiness. He writes, "Attaining lasting happiness requires that we enjoy the *journey* on our way toward a *destination* we deem valuable. Happiness is not about making it to the peak of the mountain nor is it about climbing aimlessly around the mountain; *happiness is the experience of climbing toward the peak.*"[52] An ice cream cone may perk up our afternoon. Ambitious activity, though, an engaging climb toward a valued peak, will bring us true contentment.

Unless, yep, you guessed it, we suffer from ambition addiction. The deeper we descend into addiction, the less we enjoy the mountain climb.

As *Any Day Now* encroaches upon our consciousness, it consumes us with visions of a destination strikingly distinct from our present locale. We grow obsessed with the peak and impatient with the climb. No longer do we celebrate the experience of buying, selling, painting, parenting, meditating, ministering, dating, or dieting. We grow to resent these activities; they are but bridges to our hoped-for happy endings, mere preludes to the main event. We clench our hands like Martha Stewart.[53] We scowl on the sidelines à la Bill Parcells.[54] Focused exclusively on the destination, we bleed the joy from our ambitious activities, activities that, at one time, offered us such sublime satisfaction.

Which brings us back, once more, to that swiftly melting ice cream cone, that epitome of temporal delight. Eventually, the road to recovery will teach us how to unclench our hands, release our scowls, and rekindle our appreciation for our passion projects, not simply as ambitious means to a glorious end, but as inherently pleasurable pursuits. First, however, we need to extricate enjoyment from the clutches of *Any Day Now*. We need ice cream cones, cups of tea, walks with friends, and rock and roll. We need simple delicacies that introduce us to the art of enjoyment. In every not-made-for-Hollywood moment of this imperfect journey, enjoyment's raw material awaits our discovery. We simply have to stick out our tongue, take a big lick of cookies and cream, and remember how to *Enjoy*.

Just as we can practice step one—*Slow Down*—anytime, anywhere, we can also practice step two—*Enjoy*—whenever and wherever we choose. Virtually every moment, dental procedures notwithstanding, offers potential for enjoyment. To practice *Enjoyment*, anytime, anywhere, we first stop what we're doing. We lift our eyes from our current preoccupation, beholding the moment at hand. Then we ask ourselves a simple question:

> *If I had no obligations, pressures, goals, or stress, if I had permission to enjoy this moment, right here, right now, what might I enjoy?*

If I stopped writing this paragraph, right here, right now, for example, and asked myself *What might I enjoy?* my eyes would immediately drift to the cup of tea cooling by my laptop. If I had no obligations, pressures, goals, or stress, if I momentarily suspended my writing deadline and cast my to-do list to the wind, I could, I would, enjoy taking a few slow sips of tea. I'd relish the tea's warmth washing over my dry, pursed lips. I'd savor its earthy bitterness colliding with my tongue. I'd appreciate how the liquid wets my parched throat and calms my knotted nerves.

Letting my eyes wander on from the tea, I'd also see the painting that hangs on my kitchen wall, its wild tangle of line and color inviting my eyes to dance and my mind to drift. If I really gave myself a license to chill, I could, I would, enjoy staring at this painting for a while. Then there's our upright piano, a few steps to my left. With my little Get Out of Jail Free card, I might enjoy banging out some old Billy Joel tunes. Or walking to our kitchen pantry, where, hidden on the second shelf beyond the children's reach, I've curated an impressive collection of dark chocolate. Then there are friends I'd like to call, books I'd love to read, and yoga I could practice. Hell, why stop there? I'm a freelancer. Nobody's watching. If I really had no obligations, pressures, goals, or stress, if I gave myself permission, carte blanche, to enjoy, I could chuck it all, hop in the car, and take off for a matinee!

In just a few seconds, I've brainstormed a lovely list of potential enjoyments. They vary in scope and style. They range from the sublime (chocolate) to the ridiculous (playing hooky and going to the movies). All of them, however, qualify as ephemeral enjoyments. I've omitted any pleasures that serve my larger ambition. I've even left "writing" off the list. I may love writing, but I love it, in part, because every word, every page, brings me closer to my *Any Day Now*. Rather than tackle this tendency head-on, rather than, this early in the recovery process, attempt to write with enlightened reverence for embodied journey and tempered destination, I cut myself some slack. I start with something simple. Like this cup of tea. Like the smell of incense. Like the painting on my wall.

I'll circle back around to writing eventually. For now, though, I focus on life's simple pleasures, unsullied by aspiration, unadulterated by dreams.

Some of us, our ambition-addled minds having inextricably coupled pleasure and progress, may find ourselves stumped by this brainstorming exercise. We can't conceive of enjoyment divorced from our dreams. When we look up from this book, right here, right now, when, later today, we look up from our computer screens, or from the asphalt while stopped at a light, when we behold this moment in all its supposed glory, we may be hard-pressed to identify a single, ambition-free enjoyment. Sure, a cup of tea sits by our laptop. A painting hangs on our wall. But the tea's lukewarm, hardly cause for celebration. The artwork's a pastoral print, mind-numbingly generic, and due for a dusting. We ambition addicts concocted our *Any Day Now* to avoid this banality, to extricate ourselves from mundane moments just like these. Now, on the road to recovery, we're asked to plumb the depths of the prosaic, to amplify this dirge of unexceptional detail. The task feels insipid and insurmountable, hardly a recipe for enjoyment.

To help us overcome this resistance, to assist us in identifying the moment's pleasure potential, some of us may want to adjust our inquiry. Rather than ask ourselves:

> *If I had no obligations, pressures, goals, or stress, if I had permission to enjoy this moment, right here, right now, what might I enjoy?*

We can ask:

> *If I were no longer an adult, but my childhood self, what might I enjoy?*

Young children have an uncanny ability to transform trivial moments into exuberant revelry. Through a child's eyes, a cardboard box becomes a spaceship, a pile of leaves a wading pool. Our childhood selves may not hoot over a cup of tea, but what about the jar of honey on the shelf? Or the snow outside our window? Or the infinite supply of streaming eighties hits we could, we would, enjoy blasting on the stereo while we dance and howl? Perhaps, all good and grown-up, the concept of pleasure confounds us. We're too old for board games, too responsible for cookies and cream. How might a single-digit version of ourselves assess the moment's pleasure potential? Where the adult detects opportunities for advancement, the child sees invitations to play.

Whether we ask the first question or the second, whether we assess our world with a mindset of unburdened adulthood or with the eyes of whimsical youth, the practice of *Enjoyment* requires suspension of disbelief. We won't actually believe, as we cobble together a list of potential delights, that our obligations, pressures, goals, and stress have disappeared. We won't necessarily feel relaxed and playful. The road to recovery, however, pushes us to step from our comfort zone and act against type. Just as *Slow Down* requires us, ravenous for speed, to decelerate, *Enjoy* requires us, desperate for accomplishment, to goof off. Not because we want to. But because our old routines have imprisoned us, and this new territory will set us free.

After we've completed step one of *Enjoy*, after we've paused, taken stock of the moment, and compiled a list of potential delights, we move to step two. We choose just one item on our list and, whether or not we want to, whether or not we feel like it, we actualize, experience, and enjoy. If, while sitting at home, we note that, sure, we might enjoy shooting hoops in the driveway, then, despite all our deadlines and unanswered texts, we take a deep breath, put down our smartphones, and walk outside. We pick up the basketball from its current nest in the weeds. We perform some perfunctory dribbles, all the while eyeing our neighbors' windows to see if anyone's watching. And then we, who have promised ourselves the keys to the kingdom if we keep our eyes on the prize, who once dreamed of basketball stardom before we learned we'd reach five foot ten at best, who then turned our backs on basketballs and recreational spheres of all dimensions, and turned instead to a severe and monolithic pragmatism that could, that would, any day now, propel us far higher than the rusted rim and tangled net beneath which we now stand, we, the compulsive conqueror, the ambition addict, lift the basketball and shoot.

As the ball soars through the air, as the *Enjoyment* we've chosen is actualized, we have one job and one job alone. We pay attention. We see the spinning sphere. We hear a car honk in the distance. We feel the heat of the afternoon sun. We watch the ball bounce off the boards, or swish through the net, or air ball its way into the shrubs. Then, the moment concluded, the shot taken, we can, if we like, take another shot. Or we can head back inside. As ambition addicts, we've focused primarily on quantity, on building bigger platforms, larger bank accounts, longer resumes, and more illustrious lists of accolades. When we *Enjoy*, we focus instead on quality. We're not required to belabor the point. Nor are we under pressure to fulfill a recreative quota. It doesn't matter how many hoops we shoot. It only matters that, when that ball soars through the air, we allow ourselves to experience the moment completely. We submerse ourselves in a single, pure, unquantifiable moment. We renew our spirits with one solitary shot.

By doing our utmost to relish the sensation of the basketball's leather against our palms, or the sight of the painting's vibrant color, or the explosive sweetness of ice cream colliding with our eager tongue, we do far more than provide ourselves momentary release from stressful striving. Bathing ourselves in enjoyable sensation transforms the mind, down to our very neurons. With every mindful lick of ice cream, with every basketball, specialized groups of neurons release a cocktail of chemicals, including oxytocin, norepinephrine, and endorphins. These chemicals flood the brain with the sensation we call "pleasure." Every time we mindfully *Enjoy*, these neurons grow stronger, more active, and more likely to fire in the future. In other words, when we allow ourselves to delight right now, we prime our brains to more easily delight in the future.[55] We create brains that are, bit by bit, basketball by basketball, permeable to pleasure.

When we regularly practice *Enjoyment*, when we create pleasure-permeable brains, we also receive a refreshing antidote to *Any Day Now*'s neural roller-coaster ride. Up to this point, with so little time in the day and so much to accomplish, we have likely bypassed the majority of life's trivial pleasures. For a buzz, for a fix, we've turned instead to *Any Day Now*. Forgoing all manner of ice cream cones and basketballs, we've gotten high on hope.

Like the high we receive from pleasurable activities, the high we receive from contemplating our *Any Day Now* also corresponds to a stream of neural activity. Each time we duck into that theater behind our eyes, each time we glimpse our fantastical future, this daydream triggers our neurons to release a chemical called dopamine. Like oxytocin, norepinephrine, and endorphins, dopamine provides the brain with a sensation of pleasure. Dopamine-derived pleasure, though, is frequently linked to anticipated reward—reward not in the present moment, but in a moment to come. As dopamine floods our synapses, another part of the brain, called the cingulate cortex, monitors whether the anticipated reward, the fantastical future, actually lives up to expectations. The cingulate cortex wants to know: Does our hoped-for happiness actually deliver the goods? If, over time, the cingulate cortex detects satisfaction, our dopamine levels stay elevated. If the cingulate cortex detects disappointment, however, our dopamine levels drop. We experience this decline in dopamine as the sensation of unhappiness, malaise, even downright despair.[56]

Any Day Now, as we ambition addicts know all too well, rarely delivers the goods. We picture our kids graduating as valedictorians, but even if we chain them to their desks morning, noon, and night, odds are that some of them won't make the cut. Most of our lives, we psyche ourselves up only to have our hopes dashed. Whenever we rise high on hope and come up empty-handed, we experience a short burst of dopamine followed by a prolonged dopamine decline. *Any Day Now* initially puts a spring in our step; ultimately, though, *Any Day Now* acts as a depressant. Rather than turn away from its empty promises, however, rather than refresh ourselves with an assortment of ephemeral, endorphin-infused pleasures, we ambition addicts suck it up, bite the bullet, and get right back on the horse. We force ourselves to run faster, to try harder, to ignore our growing despondency and claw all the more fervently for the stars. In a lamentable irony, we even blame current circumstance for our foul mood, growing all the more convinced of the present as prelude and the future as salvation. We deify the drug that dampens our spirits while demonizing the reality that could refresh our souls.

So, just as we practice *Slowing Down* whenever we detect our pace growing manic, we practice *Enjoyment* whenever our mood turns sour. Face frozen in a scowl? Sip tea. Hands and jaw clenched? Shoot hoops. Been painting the world with pessimistic brushstrokes for the past few hours? Eat chocolate. Play piano. Call a friend. Take a walk. On the road to recovery, we respond to ambition-induced lows not with another hit of hope, but with the analgesic of *Enjoyment.* We release ourselves from our dopamine doldrums, shining sunshine on synaptic tissue and wiring our brains for subsequent delight.

The benefits of *Enjoyment* extend far beyond a simple boost to our biochemistry. By practicing *Enjoyment* each time we drift toward despair, we continue to heal the complex of physical, emotional, and spiritual wounds wrought by our ambition addiction. Physiologically, *Enjoyment* acts in the same manner as *Slow Down*, providing release from fight or flight. Mindful *Enjoyment* signals our limbic system to stand down. Pleasure reduces the stress placed on our endocrine, respiratory, cardiovascular, digestive, and nervous systems, allowing our bodies to reabsorb stress hormones, regulate respiration, and lower blood pressure. Of course, opting too often for ice cream cones and chocolate bars will present us with a new set of health complications. If we vary our indulgences, however, taking care to sample a diversity of delights from a myriad of moments, the path of *Enjoyment* will nourish our ambition-battered bodies: neurons to nerves and blood to bones.

Enjoyment can also help to ameliorate damage inflicted upon our relationships. The more we *Enjoy*, the more our family, friends, colleagues, and neighbors will wonder, "What's going on with Dad?" When I forget to practice *Enjoyment*, for example, I find myself viciously pounding on the keyboard, aching for an *Any Day Now* bestseller, strung out from dopamine decline. In this pleasure-impoverished state, I'm more inclined, when my seven-year-old daughter, Avital, wanders by to show me her latest artistic creation, to blow her off or, worse, to snap at her for daring to interrupt the Great American Author at work on his craft.

On the other hand, when I practice *Enjoyment*, when I note my desperation and respond as prescribed, I write with a lovely brew of oxytocin, norepinephrine, and endorphins floating through my system. I feel brighter, lighter, and more optimistic. This time, when Avital stops by with her study of zebra in repose, I'm more likely to look up from my writing and smile. I'm better able, having gifted myself an earlier moment of *Enjoyment*, to bestow upon her some *Enjoyment*, as well. At age seven, Avital's not blowing bubbles like the Carnival Cruise girl and eyeing me with shoot-from-the-hip preteen incredulity. Nevertheless, she registers my response. She notes the harmony of our interaction, the affability of our shared space. Over time, my improved disposition sweetens and strengthens our relationship. It may even heal hurt caused by any earlier neglect.

Of course, just as *Slowing Down* may elicit pushback from those accustomed to a faster pace, *Enjoyment* may raise the eyebrows of no-nonsense types who view ephemeral delight as foolish indulgence. Who do we think we are, shooting hoops in our driveway while our fellow suburbanites skedaddle through their day? What do we think we're doing, taking an afternoon off to go to the movies? We can respond to the quizzical looks and skeptical queries, again, with honesty. We've been so serious and severe for so many years. We've all but forgotten how to smile. We can't remember the last time we laughed. "As odd as it sounds," we may confide, "this ice cream cone's an antidote. This movie is medicine. I need these simple pleasures to remind me that I'm human. I need these little indulgences to remind me I'm alive." Who knows? Maybe our inquisitors have sensed, in their own lives, a similar lack of *Enjoyment*. Next time, they may even join us for a nice cup of tea.

As *Enjoyment* heals physical wounds and repairs emotional hardships, as it rejuvenates and renews, it also provides us spiritual realignment. Profound contentment is not actually found in cups of tea. Resplendent joy does not really reside in ice cream cones. True happiness is the radiance of the soul, the experience of our inner light reverberating through a relaxed body, an open heart, and a focused mind. With every basketball, with every chocolate bar, with every inane delight elevating every depressed mood, we invite our bodies to relax, our hearts to open, and our minds to engage. We treat the present not as a waiting room to be endured, but as a playground to be enjoyed. We fling our bodies through that playground with abandon, reminding ourselves of what we've known but forgotten—once upon a time, we were children, wide-eyed and full of wonder. We walked the earth unencumbered by ambition. We danced and scribbled. We licked batter from the bowl. We let life rush in and thrill us to our core. Since then, of course, we've matured. We've watched responsibilities supplant recreation. Our soul, however, our eternal and ageless essence, aches for release. It yearns for another round on the monkey bars. It needs us, every once in a while, to go wide-eyed and full of wonder. So, though we could be chasing our dreams, though we should be good and grown-up, we *Enjoy* a sip of tea. We celebrate. We take another tiny, tremendous step toward spiritual well-being, edging ourselves one sip closer to the happiness we seek.

Step Three

Give Thanks

To make it through the night is a miracle. To pry open sleep-encrusted eyes and smack "Snooze" on irksome alarms is cause for celebration. In the Jewish tradition, ancient rabbis characterized sleep as one-sixtieth of death, our nightly divestment of consciousness a flirtation with the beyond. Not that we'd remember this dance with death, of course. We blacked out. We drifted through dreams. But we can listen to the stories the wise ones tell—that each night death spins us round and round, our eyes rolling back in their sockets and our mouths dropping open, our breath pungent, fungal, our snore a death rattle, a settling of bone. Most of us emerge from this dance unscathed. But the night never retreats empty-handed. A few eyes close, never to open. "Now I lay me down to sleep, I pray the Lord my soul to keep," a Protestant prayer intones. "If I should die before I wake, I pray the Lord my soul to take." To fall asleep each night is to roll the dice. To awaken each morning is to win the grand prize.

This nocturnal brush with death can guide us to gratitude. Mortality introduces us to life's true character—capricious, precarious, precious. To acknowledge the great beyond allows us to appreciate sensate existence. Simple routines become cherished gifts. We feel blessed just to open our eyes, groan, scratch ourselves, and climb to our feet.

Yet, without a practice of gratitude, without an act of thanksgiving reminding us of the void we have escaped and alerting us to the bounty we now enjoy, the miraculous can feel commonplace. The alarm sounds and we pick up where we left off, happy or sad, engaged or withdrawn, unquestionably living but not demonstrably alive. We may have the inkling that something significant took place between the close of business last night and reveille this morning, but this impression quickly evaporates, allowing us to enter the day unaware of our nightly forays and morning reprieves.

Without words of thanks, we ambition addicts create a vacuum soon filled by the expectations of ego. Our denial of death, our evasive maneuvers about *Mortality*, provide a breeding ground for entitlement and self-involvement. We give thanks if, and only if, we get what we want. We celebrate life's miracles as defined by our desire. Gratitude exists not as a foundation of awareness, but as a function of circumstance. When circumstances deteriorate, we suffer a thankless existence.

So, to deepen our wisdom and perpetuate our contentment, we practice gratitude. We *Give Thanks*. Gratitude functions, first and foremost, as an act of truth telling. When we *Give Thanks*, we tell it like it is. Life is fragile, death is undeniable, and, by the grace of God or by an act of fate or just by virtue of how the capricious cookie crumbled, we've ended up, right here, right now, topside. Phew! Worked out pretty well, all things considered. Before we get down to any specifics, before we consider any detailed evidence that might add or detract from our appreciation, we start with truth, absolute and irrefutable. Life is never guaranteed, yet here we stand. *Thanks.*

"To tell the truth, the whole truth, and nothing but the truth" takes on a special significance for the compulsively ambitious. We addicts have devoted our lives to steadfastly rejecting reality and earnestly embracing fantasy. We've constructed *Any Day Now* in opposition to truth. Our all-or-nothing futures depict us ageless, timeless, and all but immortal. Truth is a buzzkill; we'd rather live in our heads. Yet, by waging war with truth, we've created casualties of our lives. We've turned this miraculous life into an interminable struggle, a tug-of-war between perfect dreams and imperfect reality. We've cursed our own and others' fragility. We've grown vicious and exhausted. Death continues to haunt us; we sense the enemy's encroachment at every turn. Rather than consider the truth—that without exhalation, there is no room for inhalation, that without death, there is, chemically, biologically, socially, intellectually, and spiritually, no opportunity for life—we kick and scream. We scheme and strike. Meanwhile, *Any Day Now* remains at a distance. And we keep getting older. We can feel it in our bones.

When we practice gratitude, on the road to recovery, we put down our weapons. We enact a ceasefire. We shake hands with death, and by doing so, detect life's miraculous pulse. From this honest encounter with the truth of life and death, we speak truthful words. Not sentiment. Not fantasy. Truth. Perhaps for the first time in quite a while, we ambition addicts taste truth as it rolls off our tongues. We feel truth as it passes over our lips. We hear the timbre of our voices unencumbered by agenda, pretension, and fear. Over time, we, masters of the tall tale, we, authors of the conquest narrative, grow practiced in the art of honesty.

To *Give Thanks*, we can't just think grateful thoughts. We have to speak. We need to create sound. Even if we choose to whisper, we must whisper with enough strength to hear each and every word. An act of audible, intentional speech acts upon us from the outside, focusing the mind, opening the heart. As we've already seen on the road to recovery, our wild cacophonous thoughts and tangled tempestuous emotions don't always coincide with our external activity. We *Slow Down* despite panicked thoughts. We *Enjoy* in the midst of emotional malaise. First, we act. Later, we feel. Here, too, we *Give Thanks* despite our lingering skepticism. We practice gratitude even at times when we feel defeated and bereft. We don't repress thoughts and emotions, but we don't fetishize them, either. We *Give Thanks* on the good days and also on the bad, allowing words voiced without to transform ourselves within.

While the linguistically limber among us may feel comfortable launching into spontaneous tribute, some of us may appreciate having a text, a script to which we can turn to direct our thanks. For those tempted to cull a thanksgiving text from the pages of a prayer book or the wispy ramblings of a favorite greeting card, a reminder: to *Give Thanks* is to tell the truth. Words of gratitude, as they leave our lips, should sound plausible. They should strike us as something we might actually say. Sure, I could write a poem and ask you to recite it—an ode of thanks dolled up in fine, filigreed verse. But I doubt you'd own the words. We live different lives. We employ different lexicons. Rather than pay lip service to my version of gratitude, or to anyone else's, we can take some time, now, to put the truth in our own words.

To create a personalized text for thanksgiving, we start with the foundational declaration—*Thank you for life*—and ask: How would we, in our own style, with our own backgrounds, beliefs, personalities, and preferences, honestly and authentically speak these words? How do we, in other areas of our life, give thanks for exquisite, priceless gifts? Would we stick with a simple "Thanks," "Thank you," or "Thank you for life," or would we dress things up a bit? What words fit the occasion? What syntax turns the universal—*Thank you for life*—into a personal, particular blessing?

To help us answer these questions, we can take our template—*Thank you for life*—and break it down into three components:

1. Thank
2. you
3. for life

Every time we give thanks, whether to a greater power for granting us life or to a gas station attendant for filling our tank, we include some variation on these three components. First, we *thank*—we employ a word ("Thank") or a group of words ("Wow, it's so great . . .") that signify gratitude. Second, we address this thanks to a *you*—sometimes by using the word "you," sometimes with a name ("Thanks, Sue,"), sometimes with a moniker ("Thanks, big guy,"), and sometimes, when we opt for the singular "Thanks," by implication alone. Third, we designate the reason for our thanks, either by stating it out loud ("for life,") or, again, by implication ("Thanks").

Having broken down our initial declaration into its three components, we can personalize our thanksgiving text by tweaking each of these components to suit our style. Perhaps, in our own words, the first component, "Thank," will stay the same. On the other hand, we may feel more natural turning "Thank" into "I want to thank," "I give thanks," "Thank you so much," or "I want to thank you from the bottom of my heart and the depth of my soul." Maybe we want to spice up "Thank" with a favorite colloquialism or two. I might not greet the dawn with a howl of "This is the fuckin' bomb!" but if this colorful exclamation floats your one-of-a-kind boat, if this feels to you like an honest, authentic expression of gratitude, fuckin' bombs away.

After we've put our stamp on "Thank," we turn to the second component, "you." Before we get down to any rewriting here, we need to decide: Who is this "you"? What deity, power, person, place, or thing so magnanimously granted us another day on this third rock from the sun? For some, the answer is God. The "you" is Adonai, Allah, Jesus, Krishna, Buddha, Waheguru, or any other moniker for the All Knowing and All Powerful. However, if a deified "you" alienates more than inspires, the "you" could be Mother Earth, Nature, the Universe, or, and I'm definitely not kidding about this, the Force. Still not hitting home? How about thanking the all-pervasive Moment or the all-encompassing Now? How about tipping one's hat to Chance, Destiny, or the vicissitudes of Fate? We can even thank big-L Life for our little-l lives, voicing gratitude to that great ecological ocean for manifesting our tiny, cresting wave. Whatever mechanism we believe fills us with vitality, whatever power keeps us breathing through the night, allowing us to sidestep all manner of statistically plausible alternatives, that's the "you" we now turn to in thanks.

If we, on the other hand, believe that no agency sustains us, if we find this very discussion either nihilistically objectionable or migraine inducing, we can still practice gratitude. We can still thank a specified "you." When we *Give Thanks*, we can thank the Nothing. We can thank Nothing At All. In the name of truth, we honor our empirical pragmatism. We hold firm to our lack of belief. We offer oblation to the all-pervasive Absence, expressing gratitude to a "you" that, by its very nature, does not exist. Our iconoclasm may raise the eyebrow of many a theist, but no matter. For us, Nothing is the God's honest truth.

Could we skip the "you" altogether? Every Thanksgiving, for example, my family has the tradition of going around the table and, always to a few participants' thinly veiled discomfort, asking everyone to share a word of thanks. Most, including myself, answer with the preamble: "I am thankful," as in "I am thankful for family and friends," "I am thankful that Aunt Sylvia made her insanely delicious pecan pie," or "I am thankful Grampa Pete has thus far refrained from talking politics and ruining yet another Thanksgiving." Whether intentional or not, "I am thankful" defaults to passive tense, allowing us to sidestep the "you." For those of us who find metaphysical musings either arduous or insufferable, this route, at first glance, appears to solve our predicament. Rather than thank someone, or something, we can just be thankful. No god to address. No agency to acknowledge. No "you."

Served up alongside turkey and stuffing, "I am thankful" has its place. On the road to recovery, however, we ambition addicts are better served by the emblematic "you." When we say "Thank you," we acknowledge the existence of a "you" that is other than a "me." Unlike *Slow Down* and *Enjoy*, which we can practice in relative isolation, focusing exclusively on our individual speed and our personal delight,

Give Thanks involves a recipient. We address someone, or something, other than ourselves. The practice of gratitude introduces an essential concept—recovery takes place within relationship. By tempering self-involvement, we create space for transformation. "I am thankful" may plant the seed, but "Thank you" cracks open the husks of our entrenched narcissism, providing us the room we need to grow.

A name spoken aloud expresses care and consideration. We say someone's name not only to get their attention, but to intimate that we see that specific someone, that we acknowledge their unique, dynamic, mysterious, irreplaceable existence. So, while we may choose to stick with the implied "you" of "Thanks" or the simple "you" of "Thank you," we may decide, instead, to actually name our gift giver. We could, in that spirit, address our thanks not to "you" but to "God," "Creator," "Spirit," "Allah," "Adonai," "Jesus," "Buddha," "Brahma," "Gaia," "Universe," "Cosmos," or, in case you still thought I was kidding before, "Force." We could offer our thanks to "Nothing." We could also amend these names with all manner of affectionate adjectives. "God" could become "Loving God." "Creator" could become "Compassionate Creator." Even "Nothing" might turn into "Indescribable, Indefinable, Unknowable Nothing." Sprinkle to taste, if we like, with an "O" or "My," as in "O Compassionate Creator" or "My Loving God," and there you go—we have the beneficiary of our thanks, designated and detailed.

Having personalized the "Thank" and "you," we turn, finally, to the third component of our gratitude template: "for life." To personalize "for life," we continue to employ all manner of euphemisms, adjectives, and imagery. If life, in all its unfathomable complexity, strikes us as strange and amazing, we can give thanks "for this strange and amazing life." If we don't imagine life as a thing, but as a force or energy, we can give thanks "for this life force" or "for the energy that courses through my being." When life feels like a roller-coaster ride, full of precarious highs and terrifying lows, there's no need to mince words. Just put it all out on the table: "I give thanks to you, Mysterious Source of Life, for this intense, terrifying, thrilling, sometimes really hard, sometimes really good, roller-coaster ride of a life." Though we should steer clear of unequivocally negative descriptions ("Thank you, Jesus, for yet another day of misery" kind of misses the point), neither must we paint with sanguine brushstrokes. The practice of gratitude provides a floor for free expression. We can pay homage to life's bittersweet complexity, giving thanks for the ups, the downs, and everything in between.

Few of us have any experience with this kind of writing assignment. Pseudo-liturgical prose is likely not our strong suit. No matter. Just wing it for a while. Play with the words. For all three components of gratitude, for the "Thank," the "you," and the "for life," jot down lists of potential phrases. Chew on each option for a while, speaking the phrases out loud, listening for their resonance, and noticing if, after spoken, the words sink with a thud or float toward the sky. "Thank you for life" might do the job, but "I want to thank you, Holy Spirit, for the energy, will, creativity, and love that fills me from my head to my toes and from my skin to my soul" has panache! So does, for that matter, "Brahma, you rock my world—thanks for keeping me topside." With a bit of trial and error, each of us has the capacity to develop a palatable yet personally inspiring language for gratitude, a trope that, when recited, will focus our minds and soften our hearts.

On the road to recovery, we make a commitment to *Give Thanks*, at the very least, once a day—upon waking each morning. Daybreak recognitions remind us to acknowledge that cold desert of night from which we've emerged. Morning benedictions nudge us to give mortality a final nod before we charge out into the warmth of the sun. The intention is not to paralyze us with panic, but to soften us, to melt our hard-edged hubris and awaken us to the miracle of each new dawn. No matter our mood, regardless of whatever manic energy or debilitating exhaustion accompanies our rise, we make gratitude our inaugural proclamation, our leadoff pitch. Having done so, we are less inclined to take our life for granted. Gratitude at dawn primes us to greet our waking hours as a gift.

Within these parameters, we may choose to *Give Thanks* while lying in bed or waiting until we've climbed to our feet. We can wait longer, if we prefer, until we've used the bathroom and brushed our teeth. For coffee drinkers like myself, we might even hold off until we've had that first gratitude-inspiring cup, until we've given the caffeine time to conquer any lingering reticence and to elevate our thanks from bewildered groan to clear-headed confirmation.

Giving Thanks may make some of us feel vulnerable, exposed, and self-conscious. If we get up each morning with someone by our side, or, in my case, if we wake up each morning in a burrito bowl of a bed holding self, wife, two kids (who once again managed to invade this last bastion of maritally sanctified space by sneaking into our bed after we've fallen asleep), and dog (passed out in a yogalike extension enabling her to take up a space two times her body length), if we enter waking life with, shall we say, company by our side, we may want to move to a quiet, unoccupied space before offering our thanks. Weather permitting, we could even step outside. As best we can, we try to find some kind of sanctuary, a cubit or two of safe space. An appropriate setting provides us the privacy we need to speak from the heart and the silence we need to hear every word.

We begin our practice of gratitude, every morning, by giving thanks for life in general, not life wedded to any specific circumstance or detail, just simple, unadulterated life. Eventually, though, we may choose to expand the scope of our morning missives, articulating thanks for the specific as well as the generic. After whispering "You are amazing, Universe—you gave me the gift of my life, and I will always be thankful," we might decide, one day, to tack on a second phrase, such as "You are amazing, Universe—you gave me the gift of *my family*, and I will always be thankful." Notice how, in this second phrase, we've preserved our personal vernacular. We've repeated, word for word, our individualized preambles of "Thank" and "you." Without sacrificing honesty or authenticity, we simply swapped "my life" for "my family," the generic for the specific.

If so moved, we may even turn our one-liner of a gratitude practice into an evolving soliloquy of thanks. What began as "You are amazing, Universe—you gave me the gift of my life, and I will always be thankful" might one day morph into:

> You are amazing, Universe—you gave me the gift of my life, and I will always be thankful. You are amazing, Universe—you gave me the gifts of my husband, Theo, and my three beautiful children, Olivia, Clementine, and Theo Jr., and I will always be thankful. You are amazing, Universe—you gave me the gifts of my home, the food in our fridge, the money in our bank, a job that doesn't suck as much as my last job, a paycheck that pays most of the bills most of the time, the writings of Toni Morrison, the movies of Judd Apatow, the incredible stick work of hockey superstar Alexander Ovechkin, and that bakery over on Seventh Street that makes those insanely delicious blueberry muffins that I know I shouldn't eat but I just don't care because if you didn't want me to eat them, dear Universe, you shouldn't have made them so damn irresistible, and I will always be thankful.

Nothing need remain out of bounds. We can *Give Thanks* for life's glorious treasures and for life's little perks. We can allow our practice of gratitude to ebb and flow, to lengthen and contract, to shift from the undeniably profound to the ostensibly trivial to the undeniably profound once more. Each morning, we simply turn the ignition with our opening declaration of thanks, and then we see where the gratitude leads.

By giving thanks each morning, we develop a practice of gratitude that is durable and dependable. As long as we exist, it exists. No matter the state of our health, relationships, careers, or finances on any given morning, we *Give Thanks.* Even if we awake with that all-too-familiar feeling of panic and desperation, even as rage boils in our belly and *Any Day Now* shimmers behind our eyes, we put all that aside and remind ourselves that this life—this life barreling down on us right now, with its smiles, tears, triumphs, defeats, exuberant bear hugs, gut-wrenching loneliness, unbounded horizons, and unreconciled regret—this life is a gift. On hopeless, thankless mornings, we don't give in to despair. We plant seeds of gratitude and watch them slowly, surely bloom.

Will we believe any of this at first? Maybe. Will a spirit of gratitude soon permeate our sensibilities from dawn until dusk? Doubtful. With regular injections of gratitude, however, morning after morning, week after week, month after month, and, yes, year after year, we will see a change. Thankfulness will begin to percolate within. We may find ourselves inexplicably thankful while reading that God-awful book about the bunny for the thirteen-thousandth time to our kids. Goose-bump-accompanied gratitude may overwhelm us in the middle of the supermarket aisle. We start to appreciate things we would never have noticed until now—the way sunlight and shadow dance across our neighbor's porch midmorning, the sound of a friend's laughter, Joe in accounting's habit of softly whistling "We Will Rock You" on Friday afternoons. The "life" for which we've *Given Thanks* includes each of these moments and many more. With steady practice, we start to see this life with grateful eyes. By giving thanks, we start to feel with a grateful heart.

Step Four

Donate Time

Before becoming a father, I thought I would love snow days. I imagined whipping up pancakes for half a dozen chattering cherubs, then stuffing my animated offspring into cocoons of puffy outerwear and the lot of us diving from the front porch into billowing mounds of snow. We'd spend the day building forts, snowball fighting, and white-knuckling down toboggan runs, returning home at dusk to sit by the hearth, warm our frozen digits, and watch mini-marshmallows melt in our mugs. Dinner, baths, and books would work their magic, lulling our rosy-cheeked children to sleep, some not even making it to bed but passing out right there by the fire. Having carried the last of our slumbering litter upstairs, my wife and I would open a bottle of wine, cozy up on the couch, and let our gaze drift from the fire's flickering yellow to the vino's deep velvet. Then, with looks of dreamy contentment in each other's eyes, we would regale one another with tales of the day's frolicking fun.

Hence, I was shocked to discover that, as an actual father of two flesh-and-blood children, I hate snow days. The minute I hear word of an impending storm, I bristle. My stomach tightens. My jaw clenches. I seriously consider climbing into my car, pointing it due south, and flooring it until I see palm trees and retirees. As the storm looms closer, I grow feral and irritable, pacing the house, mumbling to myself, and peering outside for portentous signs of the apocalypse. When flakes finally fall, I've been known to lose it completely. Thankfully, my kids no longer need help climbing into snow pants and boots, so, as they strap on their gear and bound outside, I retreat to my bedroom, lie down on the floor, and curl into a ball. I imagine summer. I imagine sunny days and bright blue skies. I imagine running unimaginably fast across rolling hills of tall grass and wildflowers. When I dare emerge from this cocoon, I catch, out the window, ever-so-brief glimpses of our kids stretching out their tongues and running to and fro, eagerly imbibing sweet manna from heaven.

It's not just snow days that fold me into a fetal position. I panic before any school closings. I hyperventilate on the first mornings of winter vacation and spring break. I grow morose most Fridays, the weekend looming large. I secretly seethe when a kid gets the flu. I'm no monster—I worry, too. But the concerned look in my eyes, as a child's temperature climbs past one hundred, reflects both love and self-interest. I am a self divided. I love my children with all my heart and soul. But I'm an ambition addict and I work from home. A day without school, instigated by design of calendar or by dint of falling snow, is a day of plummeting productivity. A day being full-time dad requires a detour from my dreams.

We addicts love our families. We love our friends. We love our errant siblings and aging parents. We even love our incontinent pets. We may appreciate the supermarket cashier who rings up our groceries and the Starbucks barista who whips up our latte. We may feel affection for our neighbors and for fellow citizens alike. Yet, these sentient beings, of the predominantly hominid variety, have one thing in common. They don't serve our ambitious interests. They won't enable us to beat the competition. They can't help us win. True, some of them will play supporting roles in our *Any Day Now*. When we construct our triumphant tableau, we place a few of them in the frame, beaming dutifully by our side. Until that day, however, their presence, at best, serves an ancillary function. At worst, they impede our progress. We may very well love our Starbucks baristas, calling them by name, asking if they ever resolved that car insurance snafu they told us about last week, groaning about the weather, and pretending we go way back. But, come on, fellow addicts. Let's get real. When it comes to grabbing that brass ring, this assembled lot gets us nowhere. As we reach for the stars, they may as well not even exist.

Most of us keep thoughts like these hidden safely away. We would never say to a child, a spouse, or, for that matter, a kindly greeter at Walmart, "Look, no offense, but, when it comes to my all-consuming, all-encompassing ambition, you can't lift me to the stars. You won't help me get ahead. In all honesty, I'm just not that into you." While we ambition addicts refrain from speaking these words, we communicate this sentiment through a different medium. Our use, or misuse, of *time* lets others know just how we feel.

On the race to our *Any Day Now*, time is our most essential ally. Time paves the path to our dreams. More than effort, more than luck, more than all the maniacal rage we could possibly muster, time offers us true hope for success and salvation. We ambition addicts cannot physically travel from the present moment to our cherished future without the passage of time. In fact, the very words "any day now" describe a relationship in time. They provide a three-syllable surrogate for the lengthier proclamation: "There is a future, presently not the present, that will, with the passage of time, replace the present, becoming, forever, the now." Or, more mercifully: "any day now."

Time being an ambition addict's most cherished commodity, we dole it out scrupulously. We hope to receive, with every precious minute, a high return on investment. We allocate as much time as possible to productive activities. If we dream of sculpted, glistening, cellulite-free physiques, we funnel time into fitness classes and weight-lifting sessions. If we hunger for professional advancement, we pour time into early-morning e-mails, late-night meetings, and many a missed lunch spent glued to orthopedically agreeable office chairs.

We ambition addicts also allocate as much time as possible to advantageous individuals. Hoping to reign supreme over fellow parents in the carpool line, we hobnob with the heavy hitters, with the immaculately dressed, impeccably manicured moms and dads whose domestic domination might amplify our own. If we aim for pop stardom, for a Grammy on the shelf and platinum albums on the wall, we devote our time to agents, managers, studio executives, publicists, and esteemed members of the press. A minute effectively distributed to influential individuals is a minute well spent. In that minute, we've moved sixty seconds closer to actualizing our dreams.

So when the world knocks on our door, asking us in the form of, say, a snow day, to *Donate Time*, we may resist. Rationally, we get it. Snow falls. Kids stay home. Tomorrow's another day (unless, like me, you happen to live in the DC area, in which case the snow won't get cleared for a week). Emotionally, though, we feel attacked. We feel perpetually panicked and disconcertingly disembodied. We feel like Steve Jobs, who, on a luxurious family vacation in picture-perfect Hawaii, admitted, "It's hard for me. I'm always, *always* thinking about Apple."[57] Here we dive, fifty feet down, searching for sunken treasure. Now someone's come along and asked us for our oxygen tank. Can't they see? Don't they get it? We need this tank. We need this time. It enables us to strike gold. It keeps us from drowning alive.

When we consistently say no, however, when we systematically withhold our time from inopportune individuals, be they family, friends, neighbors, or coworkers, we spread seeds of suffering. By hoarding our time from the homeless veteran we see on the street corner, or from the attendant pumping our gas, or even from the family dog once again whining for a walk, we devalue these individuals. *And they know it.* They get it. They observe our indifference. They track the way our eyes look right through them, searching for someone or something more influential on the horizon. They hear the impatient disinterest in our voice, or worse, the upbeat singsong of feigned politeness, as if, with enough mindless repetitions of "That's interesting" or "How was your day?" we will have fulfilled our social contract and contributed our due. Even the thick-skinned in our midst will resent our unfavorable verdict. Our lack of care and concern hurts. Some might strike back in anger. Others will bury their resentment. Still others will grow accustomed to belittlement. They may even extrapolate from our actions, and from the callous indifference of so many others, that the entire world works this way, that not love, but crafty, calculated pragmatism, makes the world turn. It's enough to make even the dog turn cold as stone.

On the road to recovery, then, we redistribute our attention and *Donate Time*. We *Donate Time* to the people we love most in this world. We *Donate Time* to absolute strangers. We *Donate Time* when convenient. More often than not, we *Donate Time* when inconvenient. Even rushing out of the office and down to the parking garage, on a roll, in the zone, ravenous for that win dangling inches from our nose, we *Donate Time* to the parking attendant who, knowing what we do, knowing who we are, has chosen this as the opportune moment to pitch us his damn screenplay. We stand there, hot and bothered, bouncing from foot to foot, as he lays it all out—the predictable plot, the stock characters, the "interesting twist" that proves neither interesting nor really a twist. We nod and smile. We drown and die. But we don't move. Not until the five minutes once ours has been sufficiently shared. Not until we've tipped him with our time.

To practice *Donating Time*, we start by noting the cast of characters who regularly enter and exit our story. We compile a list, an actual list inked on paper or typed to cloud. On this list, we jot down the sentient creatures that play a supporting role in our story. Who do we encounter each day? Who did we bump into at the breakfast table, at the office, or in the supermarket aisles? We can omit the "extras" in our movie, such as wild animals, random pedestrians, and car-encased commuters. On the other hand, we definitely shouldn't omit bus drivers, baristas, or the attendant we see every week at the gas station. Nor should we omit toothless babies or equally toothless elders. Any regularly occurring interaction, any significant face-to-face, phone, or even online encounter, however innocuous or mundane, earns a candidate a place on our list.

As we draft this cast of characters, we should exclude anyone who moves us closer to *Any Day Now*. I have periodic phone calls with my agent and editor, but, because they service my ambition, I leave them off the list. I like my agent and my editor. We've broken bread together. We've even met each other's families. However, when my phone rings and I see one of their names glowing brightly on my caller ID, I become a teenager with a crush. My palms sweat. My mouth goes dry. I force myself to take deep breaths before answering and I never, ever, send them to voice mail. When we meet for lunch, I even change out of my standard-issue jeans and hoodie and put on slacks and a sweater. As an ambition addict with an *Any Day Now* that places me atop the *New York Times* Bestseller List, I could never deduct time spent with my agent or editor as unalloyed donation. I want them. I need them. They're my Houston, guiding me through space, enabling me to reach for the stars. When compiling my list, agent and editor don't make the cut.

For many, the individuals who serve our ambitious interests may also happen to be our dearest friends and family. Take Martha Stewart's ex-husband, Andrew Stewart, who worked as the president of a prestigious publishing house in New York. Before their marriage disintegrated, Andrew introduced Martha to the publishing world's movers and shakers, even hiring Martha to cater one of his company's high-profile publicity events. At this lavish occasion, Andrew introduced Martha to Alan Mirken, the head of Crown Publishing Group, the very same company that, five years later, would publish the first of Martha's many bestselling cookbooks.[58] Martha loved Andy, but she also relied on him. As the couple's close friend, Mariana Pasternak, writes, "Andy's sharp mind never stopped helping Martha plot her career moves." Andy proved integral to Martha's ambition.[59]

Like Martha Stewart, we may have woven spouses, children, family members, or friends into our ambitious designs. Our *Any Day Now* might even focus on our spouse's or children's achievements, their gold medals our glory, their success an extension of our own. Normally, we leave advocates and allies off our *Donate Time* list; in this instance, though, we include our loved ones' names. We are compiling a roster of potential recipients, after all, a list of individuals who might benefit from our time. Even if we've reached for the stars by standing on a loved one's shoulders, this same loved one might appreciate our time and attention, freely donated, no strings attached.

Once we've compiled our short list of names, we then note, next to each name, how we chose to spend our time with each of these key individuals during the previous day. We chart the occasions when we held tight to our time and the moments when we gave our time away. When, for example, my wife entered our kitchen for her morning coffee, did I look up from my writing? Did I pause my ambitious pursuits to give her a kiss, ask her how she's doing, and listen to a few inscrutable stories about yesterday's drama at the office? Did I, despite all my rage, close my laptop and engage? Or did I give a quick "Hey, babe," and keep pounding for that Pulitzer? At 6:13 yesterday morning, I was offered two options—donate my time to my wife, Sara, or edge a few words closer to my dreams. How did I respond? Which option did I choose?

This review of the past day's encounters and donations will likely include multiple interactions with the same individuals. We may, for instance, see our neighbor as we walk from house to car in the morning and then again as we walk from car to house at night. The cat might rub against our leg five times in one evening, imploring us to quit with the e-mails and get down to some cuddling. As many interactions as we can remember, we record, noting whether, with each encounter, we withdrew or engaged.

We may find it helpful to actually chart a previous day's encounters, using columns to differentiate between donated time and missed opportunities. My own chart of yesterday's encounters, for example, would look something like this:

TABLE 2

Donated Time—Tuesday, March 8		
Name	**Donated Time**	**Missed Opportunity**
Sara (wife)	8:30 p.m.—Watched shows, read together, and talked (90 min.)	6:15 a.m.—Worked on book instead of hanging out
Lev (son)	7:00 a.m.—Made Lev breakfast and hung out (30 min.) 4:30 p.m.—Helped him with his homework and piano (45 min.) 8:00 p.m.—Read together (30 min.)	6:30 a.m.—Worked on book instead of hanging out
Avital (daughter)	7:00 a.m.—Made Avital breakfast and hung out (30 min.) 4:30 p.m.—Helped her with her homework and piano (30 min.) 7:30 p.m.—Read together (15 min.)	6:45 a.m.—Worked on book instead of hanging out
Lola (puppy)	8:00 a.m.—Walk (10 min.) 3:00 p.m.—Dog park (30 min.)	6:00 a.m.—Worked on book instead of going for a walk 10:00 a.m.—Worked on book instead of playing or going for a walk 12:00 p.m.—Worked on book instead of going for a walk 9:00 p.m.—Too damn tired to deal with the dog
Mary (neighbor)		7:30 a.m.—Said a quick hello but didn't stop to chat 4:15 p.m.—Said a quick hello but didn't stop to chat
Parents at the school bus stop	4:00 p.m.—Talked with Jen and Yasmine about the weather (5 min.)	7:45 a.m.—Stayed in the car rather than get out and schmooze
Joel (brother)	11:30 a.m.—Talked on the phone (20 min.)	
Judy (mother-in-law)	*Didn't see Judy today*	
Mayana (yoga studio owner)	*11:50 a.m.—Saw Mayana for two minutes but she was busy checking in students*	

Donated Time—Tuesday, March 8		
Name	**Donated Time**	**Missed Opportunity**
Yoga teachers	1:30 p.m.—Thanked Carol for class and talked to her about yoga (5 min.)	
Brett (insanely buff millennial I see most days at the yoga studio)	11:55 a.m.—Chatted about the weather (3 min.)	
Sean (friend)		2:00 p.m.—Texted Sean to tell him I couldn't keep our phone date today

Once we've charted the day's myriad encounters, we scan the data. Have we fully withheld our time and attention from specific individuals on our list? Have we donated time to others, but in far lesser amounts compared with the number of occasions we rebuffed these same individuals? For family and friends who, though on our list, assist us toward our *Any Day Now*, have we devoted any time to them that didn't serve our own ambitious agendas? To practice *Donating Time*, to develop our strength and stamina in this arena, we search for opportunities to engage those we've previously neglected. We want to nourish the tacit bonds we share with family, friends, neighbors, colleagues, acquaintances, and pets. In a lovely twist of fate, the road to recovery, here, explicitly encourages our ambition. Rather than funnel this relentless drive toward a fanciful dream in our head, however, we set our sights on palpable, flesh-and-blood relationships.

Returning to my chart, I've identified two individuals (Mary, my neighbor, and Sean, my friend) from whom I withheld my time, as well as one endearingly tenacious individual (Lola, our puppy) to whom I donated some time, but not much in comparison to the amount of time she so vehemently requested. I now highlight these three individuals on my chart:

TABLE 2A

Donated Time—Tuesday, March 8		
Name	**Donated Time**	**Missed Opportunity**
Sara (wife)	8:30 p.m.—Watched shows, read together, and talked (90 min.)	6:15 a.m.—Worked on book instead of hanging out
Lev (son)	7:00 a.m.—Made Lev breakfast and hung out (30 min.) 4:30 p.m.—Helped him with his homework and piano (45 min.) 8:00 p.m.—Read together (30 min.)	6:30 a.m.—Worked on book instead of hanging out
Avital (daughter)	7:00 a.m.—Made Avital breakfast and hung out (30 min.) 4:30 p.m.—Helped her with her homework and piano (30 min.) 7:30 p.m.—Read together (15 min.)	6:45 a.m.—Worked on book instead of hanging out
Lola (puppy)	8:00 a.m.—Walk (10 min.) 3:00 p.m.—Dog park (30 min.)	6:00 a.m.—Worked on book instead of going for a walk 10:00 a.m.—Worked on book instead of playing or going for a walk 12:00 p.m.—Worked on book instead of going for a walk 9:00 p.m.—Too damn tired to deal with the dog
Mary (neighbor)		7:30 a.m.—Said a quick hello but didn't stop to chat 4:15 p.m.—Said a quick hello but didn't stop to chat
Parents at the school bus stop	4:00 p.m.—Talked with Jen and Yasmine about the weather (5 min.)	7:45 a.m.—Stayed in the car rather than get out and schmooze
Joel (brother)	11:30 a.m.—Talked on the phone (20 min.)	
Judy (mother-in-law)	*Didn't see Judy today*	
Mayana (yoga studio owner)	11:50 a.m.—*Saw Mayana for two minutes but she was busy checking in students*	

Donated Time—Tuesday, March 8		
Name	**Donated Time**	**Missed Opportunity**
Yoga teachers	1:30 p.m.—Thanked Carol for class and talked to her about yoga (5 min.)	
Brett (insanely buff millennial I see most days at the yoga studio)	11:55 a.m.—Chatted about the weather (3 min.)	
Sean (friend)		2:00 p.m.—Texted Sean to tell him I couldn't keep our phone date today

As my next step, then, I set a goal for the coming day. I choose one of these three candidates, either Lola, Mary, or Sean, and pledge to donate at least a few extra minutes, tomorrow, on that individual's behalf. In the next twenty-four hours, I must play fetch with Lola, converse with Mary, or give my old buddy Sean a call.

It doesn't matter which candidate we choose, nor does it matter how many minutes we donate or the style of interaction we employ. By donating time to one individual, we nourish that specific relationship while also developing a deeper, more comprehensive sensitivity to the role we play in all of our relationships. A chat with Mary strengthens my relationship with Mary. It paves the way for more fruitful interactions with Mary in days to come. More so, though, a chat with Mary sensitizes me not only to Mary's presence, but to Lola's, and to Sean's, and to so many others'. To *Donate Time* to Mary is to dislodge ambition's blinders from my eyes. Every minute donated teaches me to value sentient beings not for their usefulness, but for their simple proximity, for their flesh-and-blood presence on this otherwise lonely planet.

When we follow through, tomorrow, by engaging one of these handpicked individuals, we may encounter what we've likely encountered at every stage in our recovery: internal resistance. We declined this same individual the day before for good reason. He threatened to distract us from our dreams. We considered her extraneous to our striving. The following day, when we reverse course and choose to engage, we can expect, then, to feel itchy, edgy, and impatient.

The encounter might start out pleasant enough. I might see Mary watering the flowers by her front stoop, stroll over to her, and say, "Hi, Mary, nice day we're having, isn't it?" Mary might answer, "Yep, sure is." Then, remembering my pledge to *Donate Time* and embellish this encounter, I might ask, "So, Mary, how's it going?" And Mary, perhaps a little surprised that her busy, brooding neighbor would inquire so amiably of her well-being, might smile, take a deep breath, and respond:

> Well, you know, I couldn't sleep last night. So I looked outside my window. This must have been, I don't know, around three in the morning. I saw these kids, teenagers, running back and forth between our yards. Right here. Now I know your son's bike was stolen last fall. And I had a shovel and two deck chairs stolen, too. I think it's these hoodlums. They run around, high on God knows what, and if it isn't locked up, they'll snatch it. I used to work in the schools. Oh, yes, I taught history at Long Lakes High, and let me tell you, some of those kids, well, I was afraid for my safety! The girls, half of them are pregnant. The boys are in the gangs. You wouldn't think it, out here, but we've got gangs, too. A lot of these kids come from El Salvador and Nicaragua, or their parents come from there, and the gangs come with them. Such a shame. Some of them were sweet kids, but you know, they're poor and their parents are on welfare . . .

At some point during Mary's eloquent, captivating dissertation, I've started praying for a drone to copter down from the clouds and put me out of my misery. As I *Donate Time* to Mary, I can picture the pressing e-mails flooding my in-box, the unchecked tasks on my to-do list, and all the writing I've left unwritten while I listen to what's evolved into my nosy neighbor's treatise on immigration. Objectively, two minutes have passed. Subjectively, I'm crawling out of my skin. I contemplate faking a migraine or pretending I've received an important text on my phone. I thought I'd picked a quick fix. Yet, here I stand, bored to tears, eager to flee, and wishing I'd chosen to *Donate Time* by taking Lola for a walk.

When training to *Slow Down*, on the road to recovery, the practice of *Breath, Word, and Deed* left us equally edgy. *Uncertainty* and *Vulnerability* nibbled at our nerves. *Mortality* bore into our bones. Rather than ignore or repress, we respected our restlessness. We practiced *Breath, Word, and Deed* for three breaths, at first. Then, for four breaths. Then, for five. Eventually, we worked our way to twenty or thirty breaths, but we did so tenderly, cultivating our capacity with patience and care. When we *Donate Time*, when we reach out to those we previously considered tangential, we should adopt an equally accommodating approach. In the midst of a donation, if we feel resistance arise, we can casually glance at our watch, note the time, and resolve to donate another sixty seconds. When those wearisome sixty seconds expire, we should go ahead and fake that migraine, read that fictional text message, or employ whatever strategy we need to politely extricate ourselves from the encounter. Then, the next time we practice, we can shoot for two minutes. And the time after that, three. On the road to recovery, we strengthen our abilities slowly and systematically, challenging without overwhelming, growing without grinding to a halt.

As we continue in our recovery, we should repeat this exercise, ideally every day, or, at a minimum, once a week. Each time, we should list our cast of characters, chart the previous day's interactions, identify relationships in need, choose one of these relationships, set a goal for the following day, and then *Donate Time*. To facilitate this practice, I've provided a blank *Donate Time* chart that you can download from my website at www.benjaminshalva.com. Feel free to print this chart as many times as needed, or to replicate the chart in the pages of a journal or with your own database software. We should keep in mind, too, when filling in our charts, that the majority of the names listed in the left-hand column will stay the same, day to day and week to week. Our spouses, children, pets, siblings, parents, friends, neighbors, colleagues, baristas, bus drivers, yoga studio owners, gas station attendants, and insanely buff millennials aren't going anywhere anytime soon. Eventually, we may even want to tweak our personalized template to include these usual suspects, adding just a few blank rows at the bottom of our charts for guest appearances and surprise cameos.

As we repeat this exercise day after day and week after week, we may notice certain relationships starting to blossom. We hadn't called our mother in ages; now, we call her every few days. And while, at first, we may have kept our eyes glued to the clock during each call, counting down the minutes until we can get off the phone, gradually, a shift starts to take place. We grow accustomed to hearing Mom's voice, if only for a few precious minutes every few days. She grows accustomed to hearing our own. We no longer spend a phone call just catching up. Our chats deepen into discussions. We stop calling for the sake of filial piety and start calling because we want to. Even with the e-mails and errands piling up, we no longer scope out an exit strategy or pray for our cell phone to die. Our donations no longer feel like donations. We'd rather share these minutes than keep them for ourselves.

By faithfully filling in our charts, we may also notice periods when previously active relationships start to fall by the wayside. In all likelihood, this will coincide with a perfect storm of ambition, anxiety, and stress pummeling us on every front. We've pinned all our hopes and dreams on some watershed moment. Next week is our big presentation to the board. Knock it out of the park, and the corner office is all but ours. Strike out, and we'll spend the rest of our days cramped in a cubicle. So, no, we haven't had a moment free, these last couple of days, to schmooze with the neighbors or cuddle with the cat. The big game's on the line—we simply can't spare the time. Next week, no problem, we'll help little Joey with his homework. We promise. For now, though, little Joey, and all other nonessential personnel, will just have to wait.

When all-or-nothing dreams dredge up panic and desperation, which we will see reflected in our *Donate Time* data, the road to recovery invites us, once more, to shift our momentum. Just when we feel the urge to milk every minute, to hoard time for ourselves, the road to recovery instructs us not to hunker down but to reach out, to *Donate Time* in the midst of manic struggle. In every aspect of our recovery, thus far, we've encountered this brand of uncomfortable, counterintuitive instruction. On a mad dash for our dreams, the road to recovery asks us to *Slow Down*. Addiction's cycle of fleeting highs and lingering lows leaves us thankless and depressed. The road to recovery invites us to *Enjoy* and *Give Thanks*. Here, once again, when ambition addiction pulls us in one direction, the road to recovery points us the opposite way. When the pressure's on, when there just aren't enough minutes in the day, that's when we practice donating our time. That's when we suck it up and schmooze with Mary. That's when it may hurt. But that's how we will grow.

We *Donate Time* on these high-octane occasions in order to cultivate a healthy relationship with others, but, when the shit hits the fan, we also *Donate Time* to cultivate a healthy relationship with time itself. Though we ambition addicts view time as our most treasured resource, we also treat time as our most formidable foe. Time is the enemy. Time dangles above us like a noose. If we fail in our ambitious endeavors, it won't be for lack of trying. Time will have simply run out. Time will have planted one last kiss on our cheek and then bolted out the back door. Time not only pressures us from without, time assaults us from within. Every minute ages us. The passage of time erodes our strength, threatens to render us obsolete, conveys us, against our will, to those so-called golden years, to terminal dreamlessness, to the end of hope as we know it.

We ambition addicts react to this intractable adversary by racing against it. Indeed, the road to recovery's very first step—*Slow*

Down—addresses this war with time, providing opportunities for armistice. Here, again, when we *Donate Time*, when we shower time upon those who won't advance our ambition, we stop treating time as the enemy. Instead, we impose upon ourselves a revolutionary and radical perspective. We start treating time as a *friend*. We relate to time with love, care, respect, and gratitude. We appreciate time when it comes. We smile and wave when it goes. Chart after chart, day after day, we engage time with an open hand and an open heart.

As we watch this friendship bloom, it may dawn on us that, on so many countless occasions when we felt strapped for time, we actually had nothing to fear. Ambition addiction deluded us into imagining a deficit that did not exist. The sheer enormity of our ambition terrified us. We beheld *Any Day Now*'s impossible, impenetrable peak and panicked. We reached out for support and found, right there by our side, good old time, more faithful than the family dog. Yet, in our desperation, we clung to time for dear life. We sunk our claws into the flesh of minutes and moments, afraid that if we dared release our hold, or if we, dear God, gave time to another, we might tumble down ambition's mountain into defeat and despair. Now, however, we see that, after a chat with our neighbor, a stroll with our spouse, and a visit to our grandfather in the nursing home, after snow days and schmoozing, quick calls and lingering conversations, we've still got plenty of time. Another moment has just pulled into the station. Another hour's around the corner. By generously *Donating Time*, by filling our minutes with sweet, unambitious encounters, time, believe it or not, appears to have expanded in all directions. Standing in the center of this abundant resource, embraced by time as true friend, we look around, we breathe, and, perhaps for the first time in as long as we can remember, we've got time on our hands.

Step Five

Dream Anew

In the winter of 1979, Bill Parcells, then a college football coach, received the call of his dreams—a job offer to join the New York Giants as their defensive coordinator. His wife, Judy, who had followed Parcells through seven moves in fifteen years, responded with weariness and apprehension. She had graciously played the dutiful spouse and doting mother during the many years Parcells coached college ball, first at Hastings College, then at Wichita State University, Army, Florida State University, Vanderbilt University, Texas Tech University, and, finally, at the Air Force Academy in Colorado Springs. This most recent proposal, to move from college to pro ball and from the comfort of the Colorado Springs suburbs to New York's great unknown, was too much for her. "Bill," she lamented, "I just don't know if I can move again."

Parcells, however, had already shaken hands with Ray Perkins, the Giants' head coach. The matter was decided. They put their home on the market a few days later, Bill flew out to New Jersey for spring training, and Judy started packing. The Parcells family prepared, once more, for a move.

Four months later, in a surprising, unprecedented decision for the up-and-coming coach, Parcells resigned. Before their house had sold, before Judy and the girls had moved out East, and even before the Giants had suited up for their season opener, Parcells quit his first professional coaching job. He said farewell to his *Any Day Now.*

"There was nothing heroic about it," Parcells reflected. "But I figured I owed Judy one. She had been on the same Greyhound, seeing-America-the-hard-way tour I'd been on. Sometimes somebody hands you your dream and you've got to hand it right back." Parcells wept the whole flight home.

Leaving the NFL and returning to his wife and daughters, Parcells found a job selling property for a land development company. For the first time in years, he didn't have to race off to the office for early morning meetings. He no longer spent evenings and weekends at practices and games. He began eating breakfast every morning with his wife and daughters, and often accompanied them on field trips to explore the mountains around Colorado Springs. Parcells even maintained a tenuous connection to football, taking scouting notes for the Denver Broncos and providing radio commentary for high school football matches.

Parcells, however, was miserable. "I turned into a damn yuppie," he remembers. "I was dying. I was dying to coach." At first, he did his best to grin and bear it, but Judy could sense Parcells's growing angst and frustration. One night, as the couple watched *Monday Night Football* at a local bar, Judy turned to Bill and suggested that he consider a return to coaching.[60]

Freeze-frame. Zoom in tight on Parcells. Here we behold the once and future coach, having just received a midnight reprieve from the governor. Judy waved the white flag. Parcells, if he so desired, could return to the game.

One can imagine, at this moment, Parcells facing Judy yet looking past her, up and out, his eyes holding to an imagined horizon. Somewhere, out there, far beyond the suburban bar's humble brick and mortar, great hordes have begun to gather. Painted in tribal colors, they fill a massive palladium's nesting oval. Brethren chest bump brethren. Chanting and chattering, swaggering and singing, they two-fist lukewarm libations and toast imminent victory. Above, a silent, solitary blimp, tattooed with corporate logos, canvasses the high heavens. Suddenly, prerecorded fanfare erupts from the speakers, and the gladiators charge the field. Swaddled in body armor, they nonetheless move with mythical speed and formidable grace, triumphantly circling the arena, eliciting hosannas from the crowd. These hopeful contenders soon huddle around their prophet and patriarch, who, having entered the arena unassumingly, armed only with clipboard and scowl, offers his boys benedictions and blessings. Basking in the heat of flashbulbs and floodlights, coach and players prepare for the Super Bowl's opening kickoff. Any day now . . .

Zoom back out. Here sit Bill and Judy, husband and wife, nursing their drinks and contemplating their fates. Judy has just suggested Bill return to coaching. Cue Parcells. "I'm going to do it, honey," he tells Judy, "and someday I'm going to be a head coach in the NFL." Then, as if to taste the words on his lips, as if to bring himself closer to his *Any Day Now* by declaring his intentions aloud, he adds a final, solemn vow, "And I'm going to win a Super Bowl."[61]

For many ambition addicts, two, and only two, options exist. We shoot for the stars or we surrender. We go big or we go home. We see this very phenomenon play itself out in Parcells's story, when he goes from taking a knee in suburbia to sizing up the Super Bowl. As it became clear to Parcells, and to everyone around him, that life off the sidelines would not suffice, he entertained a single path forward, a royal road to redemption. Literally and figuratively, he left no room for second place. He dreamed a dream so grand, so ostentatiously monumental, that it would require season after season of bile-churning, infidelity-inflaming, family-fracturing obsession. It would require him to take the very heart he had silenced in the suburbs and sacrifice it on ambition's altar. All or nothing. Go big or go home. Either way, Parcells would wear the scowl.

Was the Super Bowl, in fact, Parcells's only alternative? Did he have only two choices: walk tall among the Giants or wallow in Colorado? What if, in fact, these options represented not two paths diverging from a fork in the road, but two extremes circumscribing a spectrum of possibility? What if, between life as a "damn yuppie" and life as a superstar, Parcells actually had numerous alternatives from which to choose—some exceedingly ambitious, some mind-numbingly prosaic, and most falling somewhere in between? Might he have found a way to honor his passion without immolating health and home?

We ambition addicts are dreamers. Dreaming destabilizes; in our stumbling, we risk hurt and hardship, frustration and failure. This same instability, however, frees us to change and create, develop and evolve. Where some see reality, we see possibility. Where some see what is, we see what could be. Our facility to dream is as much blessing as burden, as much gift as Achilles' heel. To enjoy the blessings, however, we must learn the art of imagination, the discipline of dream work. We don't need to quit dreaming; we need to dream different dreams, to direct the flames of ambition toward goals simultaneously exciting, engaging, challenging, constructive, and compassionate. The road to recovery doesn't lead us to dreamlessness. The road to recovery invites us to dream differently, meaningfully, to *Dream Anew*.

As we arrive at this fifth and final step, as we prepare to *Dream Anew*, we do so upon a foundation of *Slowing Down*, *Enjoyment*, *Giving Thanks*, and *Donating Time*. To alter our vision and direction without engaging these earlier steps would have proved impossible. Our existential angst and low self-esteem would have blocked our best intentions. Our demons, overlooked, perhaps even unknown to us, would have perverted our vision, ever so subtly turning our noblest of dreams into campaigns for gratification. A joke to this effect goes:

> A young man, raised by high-achieving parents, decides he's had enough. No more chasing grades. No more accolades. Thinking there must be more to life, the young man quits

his Ivy League school and sets out to discover the truth. His wanderings eventually lead him to an isolated ashram high in the Himalayas. Inspired by the austere surroundings and devout company, the young man burns his clothes, shaves his head, and dons monastic robes. He spends his days meditating, studying esoteric scripture, and contemplating the vagaries of human existence. His parents, having not heard from him in quite a while, grow worried. Then, out of the blue, they receive a letter from their son:

Dear Mom and Dad,

I hope you are both well. All is wonderful here at the ashram. No more chasing grades. No more accolades. I spend my days looking for truth. Plus, I have good news! The guru told me that my meditation skills have really developed. If I keep this up, he might invite me to join his elite group of senior students! Before long, who knows, he might even name me head monk!

Like the young man, we ambition addicts will continue to hear our ego's clarion call no matter the setting. We will feel compelled, by internal inclination or external impetus, to increase our speed, deplore our circumstance, harbor resentment, and withhold our time. The previous steps on the road to recovery, which we should continue practicing on a daily basis, enable us to temper fear, anger, selfishness, and self-involvement. They provide us the relaxation of body, openness of heart, and clarity of mind we need to create and actualize new dreams to come.

Dreaming Anew is not demolition work, but rather a thoughtful process of reflecting, revising, and refining. Rather than discarding our counterproductive goals, we transform them. We take our original ambition and make some minor, yet essential, adjustments. Some of us, no doubt, may yearn to start from scratch. À la Parcells, we appreciate the power and potency of an Oscar-worthy proclamation. "As God is my witness," we could imagine ourselves declaring, "I will never buy, sell, paint, parent, meditate, minister, date, or diet again!" We ambition addicts find comfort in extremes. Shouldn't we scrap our counterproductive goals, quit our jobs, change our wardrobes, dye our hair, and enact other dramatic measures to prove to ourselves and the world that we have begun a new era? On the road to recovery, however, we experiment with a different aesthetic. We explore what it would mean to dream without drama, to hope without apprehension. Dreams can provide challenges, growth, fulfillment, and contentment without sending us once more, dear friends, unto the breach.

By constructing new dreams from the fabric of the old, we will also find, hidden within obsolete obsessions, the seeds of passion and purpose. Parcells, for example, dreamed his dreams for good reason. A natural athlete, he excelled at football, basketball, and baseball, playing a starring role on all three teams in high school. He played college football for Wichita State University and was even drafted by the NFL's Detroit Lions, though he left the Lions before the 1964 opener to coach at Hastings College.[62] Parcells's Super Bowl obsession was an extension of his genuine love of the game. His foray into "damn yuppie"-hood proved unsustainable, in no small part because it relegated his passion to a parenthetical.

Like Parcells, most of us chose to buy, sell, paint, parent, meditate, minister, date, or even diet not simply to reach the stars, but because we felt called to these activities. They brought us joy. They fed our souls. They made us feel alive. It's possible, of course, that some of us stumbled indiscriminately into our infatuations. Lacking appealing alternatives, we may have turned an arbitrary exploration into a debilitating obsession. The majority of us, though, won't need to *Dream Anew* by concocting innovative ambition out of thin air. The fire of unhealthy ambition may have burned down our house and destroyed our life. Here, however, amid the ashes, we can find all the material we need to rebuild and rededicate.

To practice this final step on our road to recovery, we first need to return to our list of counterproductive goals. We may have drawn up this list when we completed our diagnostic charts back in the first chapter. There, so many chapters back, we followed the example of our old buddy Al, who had diligently filled out his own chart to determine if he suffered from ambition addiction. As you may remember, Al had segregated ambitious behavior from more easygoing activity and then listed, in the far right column, the goals underlying each behavior. Finally, he had highlighted the goals that qualified as counterproductive. Those included: *I want to take over the company and retire with billions (Consulting Goal #1)* and *I want to look like Matthew McConaughey and make women swoon (Weight-Lifting Goal #2)*. His chart looked like this:

TABLE 3

	Easygoing Behavior ***(Less goal-oriented)***	**Ambitious Behavior** ***(Big hopes and dreams)***	**Goals** ***(What do I want?)***
Professional Life		Consulting work Book project	*Consulting Goal #1:* **I want to take over the company and retire with billions.** *Consulting Goal #2:* **I want to leave an ample trust fund for my daughters.**
Personal Relationships	Relationship with wife Hanging out with friends	Relationship with daughters	*Fatherhood Goal #1:* **I want my daughters to grow up into amazing women and mothers.**
Health and Appearance	Weekend soccer league	Weight lifting at the gym	*Weight-Lifting Goal #1:* **I want a healthy body.** *Weight Lifting Goal #2:* **I want to look like Matthew McConaughey and make women swoon.**

As we dust off our own diagnostic charts (again, blank charts are available for download at www.benjaminshalva.com), we should review the criteria we used to identify counterproductive goals. Early on, we established that counterproductive behavior disregards the health and welfare of ourselves and others. Counterproductive behavior satisfies our desires and serves our egos while sacrificing our own and others' well-being. However, we also noted that, as ambition addicts, we may find it difficult, if not impossible, to honestly assess the impact of our ambition. We tend to disassociate from reality when we encounter suffering. We'd rather screen our *Any Day Now* than stand accountable for the damage we've inflicted. Therefore, to identify a behavior as counterproductive, we needed to analyze the goals motivating that behavior. Of each goal, we asked the following two questions:

Is my goal an all-or-nothing goal?

Does my goal objectify myself or others?

If we answered either question in the affirmative, the goal in question qualified as counterproductive. We could expect that behavior stemming from this counterproductive goal would also prove counterproductive, creating suffering for others and for ourselves.

By definition, then, counterproductive goals are 1) all-or-nothing goals and/or 2) goals that objectify ourselves or others. To reconstruct our goals, to *Dream Anew*, we need to address these two contributing factors. We need to scale back all-or-nothing goals, allowing room for subtlety, nuance, and modest motivation. We also need to humanize and personalize goals that objectify. By making these adjustments, we can replace overwhelming compulsion with robust inspiration. We can exit *Any Day Now*'s darkened theater and, galvanized by healthy goals, animated by productive ambition, passionately and compassionately engage in our lives.

Looking down our list of counterproductive goals now, we should remind ourselves whether these aspirations qualify as all-or-nothing goals, objectifying goals, or both. Al, for example, examines his first counterproductive goal—*I want to take over the company and retire with billions (Consulting Goal #1)*—and decides that it clearly falls under the all-or-nothing category. A number of red flags lead him to this conclusion. The phrase "take over the company," for instance, implies top-dog dominance. In Al's fantasy, Al doesn't just enjoy status. Al doesn't just wield power. Al rules the roost. His *Any Day Now* positions him as *numero uno*, an absolute authority to whom all plebeians must prostrate. Similarly, "retire with billions" smacks of all-or-nothing exorbitance. With billions of dollars, Al would have more money than he could possibly spend in a lifetime. He would rank among the richest individuals in the world, positioning himself, once more, as an untouchable elite, a god among men.

To help us determine which of our own goals qualify as all or nothing, we, like Al, should keep an eye out for any extreme, amplified, or hyperbolic language. If our goal aims for the biggest, best, highest, farthest, strongest, sexiest, most esteemed, most difficult, most desired, or most admired, it is likely an all-or-nothing goal. If we yearn for unsurpassable status, astronomical acclaim, or everlasting privilege and power, we dream all-or-nothing dreams.

On the other hand, a far-reaching objective that entails impressive challenges and promises great rewards does not necessarily qualify as all or nothing. Hence the difference between Parcells's desire to land a head coaching job in the NFL and his desire to win a Super Bowl. Certainly, head coaching positions in professional sports don't come easy. Countless hopefuls vie for a few coveted spots. One needs rarefied talent, impeccable credentials, and an abundance of ambition to be able to pace those Gatorade-soaked sidelines. Nevertheless, some individuals possess that talent, amass those credentials, and burn bright with that requisite ambition. These qualities, on their own, don't make every aspiring NFL head coach an ambition addict.

The Super Bowl, though, is the loftiest peak in professional football, both by definition and by appellation. We don't call it the Good

Bowl. We don't get excited about the Great Bowl's commercial breaks. We don't wait for wardrobe malfunctions during the Commendable Bowl, and we certainly don't let our children, ages five and two, stay up to celebrate Aaron Rodgers and the Green Bay Packers' victory over the Pittsburgh Steelers during the 2011 Satisfactory Bowl. The Super Bowl is *super*—professional football's end-all, be-all. In 1979, the year Parcells declared his intentions to win a Super Bowl, only eight head coaches in the history of the National Football League had ever lifted the Lombardi Trophy. And since nothing but all would satisfy, Parcells would have to win this all-or-nothing goal. Health and home be damned.

Having categorized his first counterproductive goal as all or nothing, Al turns to his second goal: *I want to look like Matthew McConaughey and make women swoon (Weight-Lifting Goal #2).* This goal, he soon discovers, belongs in both categories. Al doesn't just want to get in shape. He doesn't simply aim to shimmy into skinny jeans. In typical all-or-nothing fashion, Al intends to re-create himself in the image of a Photoshopped, shirtless, smiling blockbuster movie star. He hopes one day to gaze into a mirror and see, looking back, the same celebrity who has so glamorously adorned the covers of countless checkout aisle tabloids and who, in 2005, beat out the likes of McDreamy himself, Patrick Dempsey, to be crowned *People* magazine's "Sexiest Man Alive."

In addition to qualifying as an all-or-nothing goal, *I want to look like Matthew McConaughey and make women swoon* also objectifies Al and his gaggle of swooning señoritas. In one fell swoop, Al has taken his body, this glorious evolutionary masterpiece, this miraculous, unfathomably complex network of flesh, blood, and bone, and transformed it, in his mind, into an unwieldy mass of cantankerous clay. He doesn't concern himself with the health and welfare of said clay. He intends to batter his body into submission, to fire it within a kiln of calisthenics. Al has, meanwhile, applied this same crass utilitarianism to roughly 50 percent of the adult population. Every woman he meets, or at least the females he considers the least bit attractive, exist, first and foremost, to stroke his ego. Their bodies, hearts, and minds, like his own, require coarse manipulation. Al has stripped them of their multifaceted humanity; he sees them solely in two dimensions.

To help us identify any goals of our own that objectify ourselves or others, we should keep an eye out for language that controls and manipulates. Goals that objectify require us, or those around us, to act or react in a specific manner. We often use words like "be," "look like," "make," and "feel" to articulate this style of ambition. We don't just want to eat a healthier diet; we want to *be* attractive. We want to *look like* a runway model. We don't just want to get along better with our colleagues at work, we want to *make* our subordinates fall in line. We want to *feel* respected and admired. When we objectify, we frequently juxtapose verbs like these with permanent states of appearance, emotion, and thought. We conceive of ourselves and others as controllable commodities. Our words construct an *Any Day Now*–worthy tableau, filled with obedient minions playing their parts and striking their pose.

Having categorized our counterproductive goals as either all-or-nothing ambitions, objectifying obsessions, or both, we can, yep, you guessed it, draw up another chart! Here's an example of Al's *Dream Anew* chart in the making:

TABLE 4

Counterproductive Goal	**All-or-Nothing / Objectifying / Both**	**Problematic Components**
I want to take over the company and retire with billions.	All-or-nothing	Taking over the company Billions
I want to look like Matthew McConaughey and make women swoon.	All-or-nothing	Matthew McConaughey
	Objectifying	Treating my body as an object Treating women as objects

Al has listed each of his counterproductive goals in the far-left column of his chart. In the middle column, he's designated each goal as all-or-nothing, objectifying, or both. Then, in the far-right column, Al has identified any problematic components, including all erroneous language, that has led to this designation.

As we construct our *Dream Anew* charts, we can detail, as Al has done, instances when multiple components contribute to a single goal's problematic status. Al, for example, has identified two components, *taking over the company* and *billions,* that combine to make *I want to take over the company and retire with billions* an all-or-nothing goal. If Al adjusted just one of these two factors, aiming, for example, not to retire with billions, but with just enough to buy a modest condo in Scottsdale, his goal would nevertheless qualify as all or nothing. *I want to take over the company and retire to Scottsdale* still describes an all-or-nothing scenario, with Al still pining for the corner office. As each of these components independently serves an all-or-nothing agenda, Al lists each component separately in the far-right column of his chart.

We have now isolated the chromosomes contributing to a goal's abject expression. After delineating these counterproductive components, we continue *Dreaming Anew* by carefully and conscientiously replacing each problematic part. Like surgeons armed with scalpel and forceps, we excise the offending filaments and replace them with healthy, productive tissue. Every slight adjustment we now make can have a profound impact on our behavior. Just as a millimeter's turn of the steering wheel can point a speeding car toward a new destination, a minor shift in a goal's articulation can redirect us toward new patterns of sustainable, productive behavior.

First, we tackle our all-or-nothing goals. To address all-or-nothing ambition, we replace each counterproductive component in our chart with a scaled-back scenario. We hold our all-or-nothing component up to the light and ask: What would this ambition look like if I decreased its amperage? How would this dream manifest in a marginally downsized format? As opposed to *taking over the company* and banking *billions*, for example, Al might set his sights on a vice president of sales position, a few pegs below CEO, and on a commensurate salary in the mid six figures. A vice president of sales position wouldn't locate him at the very pinnacle of power, prestige, fame, and fortune, but neither would it require Al to put his tail between his legs and go home. As VP of sales, he would still enjoy an exciting, engaging, ambitious life, filled with many a Type-A opportunity to exercise power and influence. He could still afford three college tuitions and siphon money into three tax-exempt trust funds for his daughters. Plus, with his eye no longer on the Holy Grail of CEO, he could greet colleagues Tom, Dick, and Harry in the halls without waiting for one of them to plunge a dagger in his back. He could eat one, maybe two dinners a week with his family. On a good week, he might even make it home to join his wife, Val, for a glass of Merlot. Not too shabby.

Al then moves to the all-or-nothing component of his second goal—*I want to look like Matthew McConaughey and make women swoon.* Rather than asking, "Mirror, mirror, on the wall, who's the fairest midlevel executive of them all?" Al considers aiming at a more modest, less-McConaughey-focused objective. Al, for example, could set a goal to tone his upper body, trim his midsection, and lose twenty pounds. Now, we all know that even a trimmed and toned Al wouldn't survive a Hollywood screen test. Al, twenty pounds lighter, would still look like Al, complete with thinning hair, scrawny legs, and that big honker of a nose that Val reassures him looks dashing and distinguished. Nevertheless, Al, twenty pounds lighter, would feel better. His backaches would ease. He'd feel more confident and maybe even walk with a bounce in his step. And those skinny jeans? They'd finally fasten in the front.

Specificity is compelling. Our *Any Day Now* has motivated us, in part, through high-definition depictions of triumph and glory. *Any Day Now* places us against particular backdrops, surrounds us with identifiable casts of characters, and spotlights specific achievements. When we *Dream Anew*, then, we need to captivate ourselves with equally detailed aspirations and equally elaborate imagery. Al, for instance, doesn't amend his dream of corporate domination by crossing out "CEO" and inserting, in its place, "get a promotion." He aims for a specific notch on the totem pole—vice president of sales. Al doesn't replace "McConaughey" with "look better" or "lose weight." He identifies specific areas of the body he hopes to improve and establishes a precise benchmark for success—losing those tenacious twenty pounds. This type of measured motivation may not deliver the thrills and chills of *Any Day Now*'s pomp and circumstance, but, by means of its specificity, our revised agenda will still captivate and inspire.

Just as we should strive for specificity when *Dreaming Anew*, we should avoid, in equal measure, goals focused exclusively on emotions. Al, for instance, may decide that, if he can't take over the company and retire with billions, he can, at the very least, set a goal to *feel* successful, *feel* accomplished, and *feel* appreciated. If he can't look like Matthew McConaughey and make women swoon, Al might simply pump iron to *feel* confident, *feel* attractive, and *feel* fit. Such emotion-centered ambition sets us up for dashed hopes and disappointments. Our feelings, from day to day, and, for that matter, from moment to moment, fluctuate dramatically. Even a billionaire CEO doesn't feel successful, accomplished, and appreciated every moment of every day. And while I haven't checked with Matthew McConaughey for verification, I imagine he feels a great range of emotions, some occupying the confident and attractive end of the spectrum, and others of the less white-toothed smiling, gleeful variety. We can no more freeze our feelings in time than we can press "Pause" on ocean waves as they crest and crash ashore. To *Dream Anew*, then, we remove emotion from the equation, focusing instead on concrete goals and actionable aspirations.

Having scaled back our all-or-nothing ambition, we move on to examine any goals that objectify. Once again, we need to isolate and analyze each offending component. However, here we don't downsize. We *humanize*. We restructure our dreams to take into account our own and others' liberty and autonomy. We ask ourselves: How would this dream manifest independent of another's actions and reactions? How might we articulate this ambition if we allowed ourselves and others opportunities for impulsivity and inconsistency? How might we *Dream Anew*; how might we maintain constructive goals and concrete objectives while allowing space for our own and others' spontaneity, unpredictability, and freedom?

Al's goal—*I want to look like Matthew McConaughey and make women swoon*—contains two objectifying components. To actualize his ambition, Al needs to treat his own body like an object. He also needs to treat women as objects. When he *Dreams Anew*, then, he needs to find a way to get in shape without such crass manipulation. To do this, Al first addresses his self-objectification. If he no longer treats his body as a reined and muzzled workhorse, a machine into which he inputs exercise and out of which he hopes to receive tabloid-worthy sex appeal, Al could still pay regular visits to the gym. He could still hope to lose weight, tone, and trim. However, at the bench-press bar, he would no longer press until his joints squealed and tendons screamed. He would try, with every repetition, to treat his body with care, attention, receptivity, and, above all, respect. He would listen to his body, challenging it when appropriate, yet backing off before causing any harm. Al might even enlist the help of a personal trainer, exploring new possibilities for getting fit without destroying his body in the process.

Al turns, then, to his final problematic component: *make women swoon*. Al's workouts have been motivated, in part, by his hunger for power and influence. He's imagined that, after enough visits to the gym, great scores of women will be swept up by his swagger and go weak in the knees. Never mind that each woman he passes, in reality, possesses a unique and unpredictable humanity. Each varies in sexual preference, desire for relationship status, mood, and relative interest in sidling up to a married, forty-something man in a gym parking lot. To *Dream Anew*, Al needs to explore the feasibility of working out without a requisite response from the opposite gender. Can he set a goal to trim and tone without reliance on a woman's ego-gratifying reaction?

When we humanize our previously objectified ambition, we will find ourselves sometimes rewriting and other times excising. Especially if we dream of receiving another's attention, admiration, obedience, and praise, we can humanize our ambition by simply extracting this component. To address his swooning-women clause, Al gets out an eraser, taps the delete key, and takes women completely out of the picture. By freeing women from the confines of his objectifying ambition, by simply omitting them from the scope of his aspiration, Al has humanized them. He no longer requires their attention and affection to make his dreams come true.

As we edit each all-or-nothing, objectifying component of our counterproductive ambition, we may want to keep track of our revisions in our chart. The next stage of Al's chart would look something like this:

TABLE 4A

Counterproductive Goal	All-or-Nothing / Objectifying / Both	Problematic Components	Solutions
I want to take over the company and retire with billions.	All-or-nothing	Taking over the company Billions	**Vice president of sales** **Mid-six-figure salary**
I want to look like Matthew McConaughey and make women swoon.	All-or-nothing	Matthew McConaughey	**Tone upper body** **Trim midsection** **Lose twenty pounds**
	Objectifying	Treating my body as an object	**Listening to my body to protect myself from injury** **Working with a personal trainer**
		Treating women as objects	**(Take women's reactions out of the equation)**

With components corrected and solutions articulated, we can now rewrite our goals. Taking each scaled-back, humanized solution from the far-right column of our charts, we insert this language into our original framework. Al's consulting goal—*I want to take over the company and retire with billions*—could now read: *I want to get promoted to vice president of sales and earn a mid-six-figure salary.* Al's weight-lifting goal—*I want to look like Matthew McConaughey and make women swoon*—could become: *I want to tone my upper body, trim my midsection, and lose twenty pounds by lifting weights carefully and working with a personal trainer.* Al completes his dream work by inputting these refurbished goals into his chart:

Table 4B

	All-or-Nothing / Objectifying / Both	Problematic Components	Solutions	Productive Goal
I want to take over the company and retire with billions.	All-or-nothing	Taking over the company	Vice president of sales	**I want to get promoted to vice president of sales and earn a mid-six-figure salary.**
		Billions	Mid-six-figure salary	
I want to look like Matthew McConaughey and make women swoon.	All-or-nothing	Matthew McConaughey	Tone upper body Trim midsection Lose twenty pounds	**I want to tone my upper body, trim my midsection, and lose twenty pounds by lifting weights carefully and working with a personal trainer.**
	Objectifying	Treating my body as an object	Listening to my body to protect myself from injury Working with a personal trainer	
		Treating women as objects	(Take women's reactions out of the equation)	

As we turn counterproductive delusions into productive dreams, when we transform outmoded fantasy into actionable aspiration, we exit *Any Day Now*'s darkened theater and reinvest in reality. The road that extends before us, when we *Dream Anew*, no longer ends at some otherworldly oasis. The path we now travel, in fact, doesn't end at all. True, we designed our new and improved dreams for realization. With achievable items on our agenda, we may, one day soon, get that promotion. We may look down at the scale, past our noticeably diminished paunch, and see that we dropped those twenty pounds. Some folks, at this point, might say to themselves, "Enough," and downshift into maintenance mode. With a promotion under their belt, a belt notched significantly tighter thanks to those vanquished twenty pounds, they might dispense with ambition. Or, to be more accurate, they might ambitiously pursue the status quo. Not us, my dear addicts, not us. We have hunger in our bellies. We have fire running through our veins. We, who once grasped at fame, fortune, conquest, and domination, we need to dream. We may have exited *Any Day Now*'s theater, but we still need heights to conquer. We still need dragons to slay.

Each time we ambition addicts turn revised dreams into accomplished reality, we will need, once more, to *Dream Anew*. We can do this by building upon a recently achieved goal, by turning one promotion into a platform for the next or by taking our toned body to the track to train for that half marathon. We can also *Dream Anew* by widening our vision, by allowing our ambition to spread to new and novel areas of our life. After stenciling "Vice President of Sales" on his door, Al may reach for a yet-higher rung on the corporate ladder. However, he may decide to finally glue his butt to a chair and write that book. He may even decide to rekindle the home fires with Val, setting goals for a once-a-day chat, a once-a-week date night, and a once-a-year couple's adventure across the globe.

While some will surely appreciate our scaled-back, humanized, and potentially diversified vision, others may object. How dare we turn off the computer and head home from the office when items on our to-do list still linger? Are we sure we want to give our kids an afternoon off from extracurricular activities when they could be drilling and developing, edging ever closer to that Ivy League acceptance? How can we settle for midlevel mediocrity when elite excellence remains within reach? As we've responded to such objections before, so we answer now. To those who object, we speak honestly. We share how the blazing fire of ambition has singed us, leaving us, and so many around us, heavyhearted and resentful. We communicate our wish to live a life of health, happiness, and hope. We also learn to accept the fact that some will remain unconvinced. Some will continue to respond to our recovery with skepticism and recrimination. In this respect, it will help to keep in mind that, in a world obsessed with fame and fortune, accomplishment and accolades, we've adopted a countercultural stance. We've conveyed, through our actions, a different set of values. Our belief in balance may, at times, place us on the margins, especially if we've surrounded ourselves, until now, with individuals equally beholden to the ego's demands. The road to recovery takes courage, the courage to stand apart, the courage to act compassionately in a world that favors fire.

The key for us dreamers is that we continue to dream. *Any Day Now* had promised us a grand finale, a final curtain call. When we *Dream Anew*, we forgo the fireworks and fanfare. We dispel the notion of an end altogether. Nice and slow, with gratitude and joy, taking plenty of breaks for family, friends, colleagues, and community, we dream our dreams and then get down to work. We labor for that promotion. We get our butts to the gym. We don't allow the fire of ambition to consume us, but neither do we extinguish its flame. Our life takes on the luster of a slow burn; we don't explode like a star, full of searing heat and blinding light. Our ambition, once a debilitating addiction, shines like a lantern, lighting our way.

Afterword

"We like the chapters you sent. We want to publish the book. But we need you to get us a draft of the manuscript in three months."

I can't think of what to say. I wonder if my editor can hear my heart palpitations over the phone. I feel dizzy and ecstatic. I stand frozen in abject terror. I stare out the window. A bland winter day stares back, stoically indifferent.

"I realize it's a tight deadline," my editor continues, "but if you think you can finish the book by the spring, we're ready to make this happen."

A writer more grounded and confident, more savvy and sophisticated, less eager to please and with far less to prove, might have answered back, in steady, sauntering baritone, "I'm deeply honored. Thank you for this opportunity. However, I can no more accelerate my craft than the cherry tree can compel its buds to prematurely bloom." Or something to that effect.

But I am not that writer. I am not that man. My name is Benjamin Shalva and I am an ambition addict. My *Any Day Now* depicts me topping bestseller lists, teaching sold-out seminars, and enjoying the type of widespread appeal and ubiquitous respect normally reserved for the likes of Oprah and the Dalai Lama (not necessarily in that order). As an ambition addict, albeit an addict in recovery, I get high when a publisher says, "We want your book." I splash into a baptismal font of adrenaline at the prospect of publication. At the mere mention of contracts, advances, book galleys, and publicity tours, dopamine stretches my grin ear to ear. In a tremulous tenor, then, I answer my editor with a gushing ramble, attempting to sound cool, forgetting to breathe, eventually petering out with a final few *Thank-yous* and *Awesomes* before she compassionately curtails my chatter.

And that, my friends, is how I signed on to write a book about ambition addiction under the weight of a very ambitious deadline. That is why, throughout the writing process, I have encountered all manner of diabolical demons, bewitching temptations, and itchy, edgy, suffocating, exasperating anxiety. I have had to practice *Breath, Word, and Deed* constantly, inhaling and thinking to myself, "I am opening my computer," exhaling and thinking, "I am putting fingers to the keys." Especially on days when, after hours in front of the screen, my eyes sting, my head throbs, and the writing refuses to flow, I've forced myself to *Enjoy* mug after mug of hot tea and bar after bar of dark chocolate. Even on those gray winter mornings when, utterly exhausted, I wanted nothing more than to crawl back in bed and wait out the thaw, I've climbed out of bed and *Given Thanks* for my life.

One especially memorable morning, I set my alarm for five to put in an extra hour of writing before the kids got up. My daughter, a light sleeper, stumbled out of bed a few minutes after me. She ambled downstairs, pajama clad and bed headed, groggy and grumpy, then tugged at my sleeve and grumbled, "Breakfast." I kept right on writing. She tugged again. "Breakfast." I muttered something like "You know where the cereal is," and kept tap tap tapping. She whined once more, this time at full volume, "Abba! I'm hungry! I want breakfast!" I took a deep breath. I turned to her and, trying to keep my cool, said, "Honey, it's five in the morning. This is my work time. If you want some breakfast, go get it yourself. I'm sorry, but I have to write." Then I turned back to the computer. I reread the sentence I had just finished writing before I was so rudely interrupted. It read: *When the pressure's on, when there just aren't enough minutes in the day, that's when we practice donating our time.*

I took another deep breath. I closed the computer. I walked over to my daughter, who had mangled a new cereal box into submission and was now enjoying fistfuls of Cheerios right from the bag. I gave her a hug. I gave her a kiss. I took the box from her, got out a bowl, and filled it with Cheerios. Seething with ambition, aching to run back to the keyboard, I then sat down with my girl and watched her finish her first round of requisite carbs.

Writing *Ambition Addiction* under an ambitious deadline was a blessing. I practiced dancing with my demons. I learned to breathe in the midst of pressure and panic. I found new wellsprings of courage, compassion, patience, and presence. I enjoyed the work and I relished the adventure. Writing *Ambition Addiction* under an ambitious deadline also reminded me that what I am asking you to join me in doing is hard work. We ambition addicts have spent a lifetime honing strategies and developing coping mechanisms for getting by on this tenuous planet. Our habitually counterproductive behavior, our self-serving rage, has left physical, emotional, and spiritual damage in its wake; yet, it is what we know. We have practiced ambition addiction day in and day out for a great many years.

Imagine a giant wheel, a wheel set in motion long ago that now spins with tremendous force. Every time we *Slow Down*, *Enjoy*, *Give Thanks*, *Donate Time*, and *Dream Anew*, we attempt to grab hold of this wheel and reverse its direction. We try to upend an eternity of speed, severity, entitlement, self-absorption, and delusion. We should expect, then, as we grip this wheel and collide with its colossal weight and seemingly unstoppable momentum, to feel frustrated and exhausted. We should anticipate confusion, exasperation, disappointment, and doubt. The road to recovery will call upon all reserves of strength, courage, patience, and perseverance. Reaching for the stars may be hard. The road to recovery is harder.

I offer these practices to you not as Sisyphean persecution, however, but as a pathway to liberation. Freedom from unfettered ambition begins by growing intimate with our own resistance, by discovering every unseemly detail of our seemingly interminable neurosis. Every time we try to *Slow Down* but, too frightened of the consequences, maintain our manic pace, every time we feel hollow and disingenuous *Giving Thanks* for a life that won't measure up to expectations, every time we tell our sons and daughters to take a hike so we can get back to our monumentally important agendas, we do so, on the road to recovery, with awareness. This road to recovery has not delivered us from slavery to freedom, not yet. But it has opened our eyes. We see our body bound and shackled, our head awash in feverish fantasy. We sense the shell, cold and brittle, that slowly but surely encases our beating heart.

We may labor like this for a while, practicing our recovery exercises, filling in our charts, encountering fear and fragility, and, more often than not, falling short. At times, we may feel that nothing will ever change. We've laid out our garden and carefully planted our seeds. We've raked and hoed, watered and mulched. Still, nothing sprouts. If we can stick with the program, at this point, practicing with patience, laboring without expectation of advancement, somewhere, deep beneath the soil, our seeds will start to stir. They just need time. We just need time. We need time to detox. We need time to heal. How long have we chased that throne? How long have we spun that wheel? Ten years? Twenty? As long as we can remember? Is it any wonder, then, that we can't just breathe, we can't slow down, we can't enjoy, we can't turn on a dime? Is it any wonder that we keep falling down?

Some of us, of course, will play at recovery. Some of us, deep down, do not want to change. Some will walk the road to recovery half-heartedly for a while, then shrug their shoulders and default to old dependencies. For those who feign sincerity, for those who practice listlessly, no amount of waiting will help. The seeds of change will never sprout. The wheel will never slow. For those of us, on the other hand, who have reached a point of desperation, who've sensed our body's collapse, who've watched our loved ones depart, who've forgotten what it feels like to explode with joy from head to toe, we must stick with the program. For those who suspect that, if we don't make a change, we will look back on our life with soul-crushing regret and immeasurable sorrow, our dogged determination will not be in vain.

Every time we fall down and get right back up again, every time we refuse to give up on ourselves and our capacity to heal, we loosen ambition addiction's shackles. We do so by reimagining success, by redefining greatness. In the past, we had conceived of success as high peaks conquered and high marks acquired. We had taken for granted that the great must earn their rank through their own and others' suffering and subjugation. Now, on the road to recovery, we learn that genuine success and true greatness have little to do with fame, fortune, validation, and praise. When we stop running from our problems, this is genuine success. When we turn to face our demons, whether or not we can withstand their punishing proximity, this is true greatness. We may still feel stuck. We may still feel enslaved. But we are learning to believe in ourselves. We are learning to love ourselves. This new appreciation, more so than any proof of progress, releases us from our chains.

On the road to recovery, on the path to liberation, we begin with self-knowledge. We continue by building self-confidence and self-acceptance, by turning from greatness without to greatness within. Then, as the days turn to weeks, the weeks to months, the months to years, we look back to discover: We've changed. We've grown. When we sense panic rising, we instinctively take a breath and *Slow Down.* We eagerly *Enjoy* life's bounty, gifts great and small. Without prompting, we *Give Thanks.* Sure, we still get hot and bothered when talking to our editor. We still bang our heads against the wall when, hard at work, our daughter demands breakfast.

Yet, more often than not, we close our computers and fill cereal bowls. We choose hope over lamentation and faith over fear. As love expands, enslavement ends.

As for our dreams, these, too, will evolve. We *Dream Anew,* at first, by turning from CEO to VP. We aim for a winning season as opposed to the Super Bowl. Eventually, though, the very character of our dreams may start to shift. We may start dreaming, not only of little leaps forward, of promotions earned and advancements achieved, but also of turning our very life into a blessing, of offering our hurt and healing to others in need.

Mesmerized by *Any Day Now,* I hoped to write a bestseller. Then, on the road to recovery, my dreams evolved. I found myself aiming for a beautiful book, a powerful book, a book rich in substance, a book filled with wise words. As I pen these final pages, I see that my dream has shifted once more. I write this book not for status, nor even for substance. I write this book for me and for you, yes, you—all of you who, like me, struggle and strive. I have labored to share with you my port in the storm.

Perhaps your dreams, too, will unfold in this direction. Perhaps you, too, will serve as sponsor to other addicts in need. As we develop our capacities to *Slow Down*, *Enjoy*, *Give Thanks*, *Donate Time*, and *Dream Anew*, others may start to notice. They may observe us, out of the corner of their eye, as we stop and smell the flowers, as we patiently push our child on the swings, as we manage, miraculously, to keep our cool in tough situations, and as we aim for lofty heights without losing the ground beneath our feet.

These same individuals may one day approach us, seeking our counsel, asking our advice, and, if we feel comfortable doing so, we may decide to share our story. I am an ambition addict, we can explain. I, too, have suffered. I, too, have struggled. I, too, have tasted loss and loneliness. I, too, bear the burden of regret. But I have also closed the computer and poured my daughter a bowl of Cheerios. I have awoken in fear yet found words of thanksgiving. I have learned, breath by breath, that this story of ours is just beginning, that each day we can choose anew.

Then, when we feel ready, we can invite others to join us on this road to freedom. The road, we can explain, twists and turns. We'll make strides forward. We'll stumble and fall. With each other by our side, however, we can transform the ache of our addiction into the gift of fellowship. Together, we will, any day now, find the freedom we seek.

To find out more about Benjamin Shalva and access downloadable worksheets related to the exercises and tools discussed in this book please visit www.benjaminshalva.com.

NOTES

NOTES

1 Interview on *Good Morning America*, February 28, 2011.

2 Charles Dickens, *A Christmas Carol.*

3 For more on my spiritual guide bona fides, pick up a copy of my first book, *Spiritual Cross-Training: Searching Through Silence, Stretch, and Song* (Grand Haven, MI: Grand Harbor Press, 2016).

4 Andrew Dice Clay, "Mother Goose," *Dice*, American Records, 1989.

5 Larry A. Thompson, *Shine: A Powerful 4-Step Plan for Becoming a Star in Anything You Do* (New York: McGraw-Hill, 2004), 32.

6 Ibid., 78.

7 Herbert Benson, MD, *The Relaxation Response* (New York: Harper-Torch, 2000), 41.

8 Gabor Maté, MD, *When the Body Says No: Understanding the Stress-Disease Connection* (Hoboken, New Jersey: John Wiley & Sons, Inc., 2003), 89.

9 Benson, *The Relaxation Response*, 52.

10 Ibid., 21–24.

11 Ibid., 30–31.

12 Herbert Benson, MD, and William Proctor, JD, *Relaxation Revolution: Enhancing Your Personal Health Through the Science and Genetics of Mind Body Healing* (New York: Scribner, 2010), 23; Maté, *When the Body Says No,* 97, 190.

13 Maté, *When the Body Says No*, 28–36.

14 Ben Volin, "Evidence that coaching in NFL is no health club," *Boston Globe*, November 10, 2013.

15 Ibid.

16 Michael Lewis, "What Keeps Bill Parcells Awake at Night," *New York Times*, October 29, 2006.

17 Luke Kerr-Dineen, "The Forty-Eight Greatest Quotes about Winning," *USA Today*, February 9, 2016, http://ftw.usatoday.com/2016/02/best-sports-quotes-about-winning.

18 Byron J. Richards, "New Insights on How Stress Causes Acid Indigestion," www.wellnessresources.com, September 29, 2011; Lewis, "What Keeps Bill Parcells Awake at Night."

19 Bill Parcells and Nunyo Demasio, *Parcells: A Football Life* (New York: Three Rivers Press, 2015), 194–204.

20 Michael Fulmore, *Unleashing Your Ambition* (New York: Morgan James Publishing, 2013), Kindle Edition, location 1323.

21 Parcells and Demasio, *Parcells: A Football Life*, 425–27.

22 Ibid., 339–40.

23 Ibid., 425–27.

24 Walter Isaacson, *Steve Jobs* (New York: Simon & Schuster, 2011), 103.

25 Karen Blumenthal, *Steve Jobs: The Man Who Thought Different* (New York: Feiwel and Friends, 2012), 136.

26 Brent Schlender and Rick Tetzeli, *Becoming Steve Jobs: The Evolution of a Reckless Upstart into a Visionary Leader* (New York: Crown Business, 2015), 79.

27 Ibid., 119.

28 Ibid., 57.

29 Isaacson, *Steve Jobs,* 565.

30 Schlender and Tetzeli, *Becoming Steve Jobs,* 41.

31 Isaacson, *Steve Jobs,* 103.

32 Ibid., 88.

33 Ibid., 259.

34 Chrisann Brennan, *The Bite in the Apple: A Memoir of My Life with Steve Jobs* (New York: St. Martin's Press, 2013), 228.

35 Blumenthal, *Steve Jobs*, 85.

36 Isaacson, *Steve Jobs,* 119.

37 Schlender and Tetzeli, *Becoming Steve Jobs,* 63.

38 Brennan, *The Bite in the Apple*, 198.

39 Ibid., 198.

40 Schlender and Tetzeli, *Becoming Steve Jobs*, 62–63.

41 Brennan, *The Bite in the Apple*, 230.

42 Ibid., 206, 258.

43 Isaacson, *Steve Jobs*, 315.

44 Blumenthal, *Steve Jobs*, 251.

45 Isaacson, *Steve Jobs*, 91.

46 Christopher Byron, *Martha Inc.: The Incredible Story of Martha Stewart Living Omnimedia* (Hoboken, New Jersey: John Wiley & Sons, Inc., 2002), 72.

47 Mariana Pasternak, *The Best of Friends: Martha and Me* (New York: HarperCollins e-books, 2010), 142.

48 Ibid., 75, 179, 286.

49 Ibid., 54.

50 Byron, *Martha Inc.*, 101.

51 Ibid., 194, 170, 282.

52 Tal Ben-Shahar, PhD, *Happier* (New York: McGraw-Hill, 2007), 27 (Ben-Shahar's italics).

53 Pasternak, *The Best of Friends*, 54; Byron, *Martha Inc.*, 170.

54 Lewis, "What Keeps Bill Parcells Awake at Night."

55 Rick Hanson, PhD, with Richard Mendius, MD, *Buddha's Brain: The Practical Neuroscience of Happiness, Love, and Wisdom* (Oakland, CA: New Harbinger Publications, 2009), 38.

56 Ibid., 37–38.

57 Blumenthal, *Steve Jobs*, 251.

58 Byron, *Martha Inc.*, 89–90.

59 Pasternak, *The Best of Friends*, 82.

60 Parcells and Demasio, *Parcells: A Football Life*, 66–71.

61 Ibid., 71.

62 Ibid., 25.

Acknowledgments

Thank you to the dream team, the collective of incredibly supportive, smart, savvy, patient, and compassionate professionals who have nudged and nurtured this book to publication. Thank you to my agent, Priya Doraswamy, for your intelligent counsel, assertive advocacy, and steady encouragement. Thank you to Erin Mooney and Sarah Faulkner, my editors at Grand Harbor Press, for asking important questions, providing helpful answers, and offering an expert eye to every line of this text. Thank you to Tiffany Pokorny, Marlene Kelly, and the entire team at Grand Harbor Press for continuing to guide me through the wilds of the publishing world. Thank you also to Julie Schoerke, Marissa Decuir, Chelsea Apple, and JKS Communications for steering the publicity for this book and for teaching me how to more effectively deliver my voice to those who would listen.

Thank you to so many wonderful friends who have encouraged me as I pound the keys. In particular, I want to thank Sean Armstrong, Ben Toth, Norman Lasca, Mat Tonti, Julie "J-Rez" Tonti, Greg Litcofsky, Rachel Litcofsky, Scott Perlo, Yael Bromberg, Judith Rosenbaum, Or Rose, Devora Rohr, Stephanie Rohr, Daniel Klein, Graham Hoffman, Sarah Tasman, Kyle Hathaway, Rachel Meytin, Sarah Meytin, Lauren Holtzblatt, Gil Steinlauf, Kerrith Rosenbaum, David Polonsky, Diane Thompson, Patricia deGuzman, Chris Grosso, Art Green, Waylon Lewis, and Rick Jarow. Your love, laughter, and steady support remind me to breathe deep, keep it light, relax, and smile. Thank you to the Bikram Yoga Reston crew for helping me sweat it out every day at noon. Thank you also to Lee Trepeck, Robin Trepeck, Debbie Landau, Sean Morgan, Carly Weinstock, Roberta Blumberg, Katy Levinson, Tomer Moked, Kitty Phillips, Rachel Devries, and the entire Tamarack Camps organization for being such incredible cheerleaders and for offering, every summer, a healthy hiatus from writing and a home away from home.

Thank you to my family. Thank you to Steve Engel, Tracie Engel, Michael Schudson, Julia Sonnevend, Benjamin Barokas, Sara Barokas, Tom Engel, Enid Sperber, Benjamin Sperber, and Suzie Schudson for your active support and for all the free PR. Thank you to Judy Barokas, my mother-in-law and editor-in-law, for your unflagging love and enthusiasm, and for editing the early drafts of this book. Thank you to my brother and sister-in-law, Joel Schudson and Zoe Florence, for your love, for believing in me, for so many good talks and strategy sessions over the phone, and for so many incredible Greenpoint hipster-brewed cappuccinos. Thank you to my parents, Charlie and Karen Schudson, for your boundless love. You have always reminded me to temper ambition with empathy. You have always encouraged me to strive for greatness without while also attending to greatness within. And thank you to my wise and wonderful wife and partner, Sara Shalva, and to my children, Lev and Avital. I get lost in my head. I wander in dreams. You wake me up. You bring me home. You open my heart.

ABOUT THE AUTHOR

Photo © 2015 Eric Kemp

As a rabbi, writer, and yoga instructor, Benjamin Shalva leads spiritual cross-training seminars and workshops around the world. He received his rabbinical ordination from the Jewish Theological Seminary in New York City and his yoga teacher certification from the Yogic Physical Culture Academy in Los Cabos, Mexico. Shalva serves on the faculty at the Jewish Mindfulness Center of Washington and leads musical prayer services for the Sixth & I Historic Synagogue and Bet Mishpachah in Washington, DC. He also serves as the camp rabbi and director of Jewish life for Tamarack Camps in Detroit, Michigan. His writings have been published in the *Washington Post*, *Elephant Journal*, and *Spirituality & Health* magazine. Born in Milwaukee, Wisconsin, he lives in Reston, Virginia, with his wife and their children.